Armored, Plated, and Bone-Headed Dinosaurs

Titles in THE DINOSAUR LIBRARY Series

THE DINOSAUR LIBRARY

Armored, Plated, and Bone-Headed Dinosaurs
The Ankylosaurs, Stegosaurs, and Pachycephalosaurs

Thom Holmes and Laurie Holmes

Illustrated by Michael William Skrepnick

Series Advisor:
Dr. Peter Dodson
Professor of Veterinary Anatomy and Paleontology,
University of Pennsylvania
and
co-editor of *The Dinosauria*,
the leading reference used by dinosaur scientists

Enslow Publishers, Inc.

40 Industrial Road	PO Box 38
Box 398	Aldershot
Berkeley Heights, NJ 07922	Hants GU12 6BP
USA	UK

http://www.enslow.com

Library of Congress Cataloging-in-Publication Data

Holmes, Thom.
    Armored, plated, and bone-headed dinosaurs: the ankylosaurs, stegosaurs, and
pachycephalosaurs / Thom Holmes and Laurie Holmes; illustrated by Michael
William Skrepnick.
       p. cm. — (The dinosaur library)
    Includes bibliographical references and index.
    ISBN 0-7660-1453-3
    1. Ankylosaurs—Juvenile literature. 2. Stegosauridae—Juvenile literature.
3. Pachycephalosauridae—Juvenile literature. [1. Ankylosaurus. 2. Stegosaurus.
3. Pachycephalosaurus. 4. Dinosaurs.] I. Holmes, Laurie. II. Skrepnick, Michael
William, ill. III. Title.
    QE862.O65 H64   2001
    567.915—dc21

                             00-011835

To Our Readers:
We have done our best to make sure all Internet addresses in this book were active and appro-
priate when we went to press. However, the author and the publisher have no control over
and assume no liability for the material available on those Internet sites or on other Web
sites they may link to. Any comments or suggestions can be sent by e-mail to
comments@enslow.com or to the address on the back cover.

Illustration Credits: Michael William Skrepnick. Illustration on p. 53 (top) after
Sereno and Zhiming, 1992 and Marsh, 1887.

Photo Credits: © Corel Corporation, pp. 15, 75, 93, 97; © Digital Vision, Ltd.,
p. 35; Wayne Grady, p. 6 (Thom Holmes); Shaina Holmes, p. 6 (Laurie Holmes);
Thom Holmes, p. 24; Thom Holmes (from the collection of the American
Museum of Natural History), pp. 40, 51, 58; Thom Holmes (from the collection
of the Denver Museum of Nature and Science), pp. 55, 56, 87; Michael Tropea, p. 7.

Cover Illustration: Michael William Skrepnick

A special thanks to paleontologist Kenneth Carpenter of the Denver Museum of
Nature and Science for reviewing the manuscript of this book.

CONTENTS

ABOUT THE AUTHORS

Thom Holmes is a natural history writer specializing in dinosaur science. He has dug for dinosaurs with leading paleontologists in the United States and South America. He has collaborated with Dr. Peter Dodson on several dinosaur-related projects during the past fifteen years.

Laurie Holmes is a science writer and editor, as well as a reading specialist. It has been her privilege to associate with many of the world's leading dinosaur scientists and artists through her work with her husband, Thom. Originally a teacher, she maintains that she is still teaching by writing and editing books for young adults.

On a dig in Patagonia, Thom Holmes holds part of the skull bone of what is currently known as the largest meat-eating dinosaur ever.

Thom Holmes

Laurie Holmes

AUTHORS' NOTE

Dinosaurs hold a special fascination for people all over the world. In writing *The Dinosaur Library*, we enjoyed sharing the knowledge that allows scientists to understand what dinosaurs were really like. You will learn about the differences that make groups of dinosaurs unique, as well as the many similarities that dinosaurs shared.

The Dinosaur Library covers all the suborders of dinosaurs, from the meat-eating theropods, such as *Tyrannosaurus rex*, to the gigantic plant eaters. We hope you enjoy learning about these fascinating creatures that ruled the earth for 160 million years.

ABOUT THE ILLUSTRATOR

Michael William Skrepnick is an established paleo artist with a lifelong interest in dinosaurs. He has worked on newly described dinosaurs with a number of the world's leading paleontologists. His original artworks are found in a number of art collections and reproduced as museum murals, and in popular books, magazines, scientific journals, and television documentaries. Michael lives and works in Alberta, Canada, close to some of the richest Upper Cretaceous dinosaur fossil localities in the world.

✦ ✦ ✦

Paleo art is a field devoted to the reconstruction and life restoration of long extinct animals and their environments. Since we cannot observe dinosaurs (other than living birds) in nature, we may never truly know their habits, lifestyles, or the color of their skin. In addition, the fossil record provides only a fraction of the remains of a wide diversity of life on earth.

Many fairly complete skeletons of dinosaurs have been unearthed in recent history. Others are represented by as little as a fragment of a single fractured bone, an isolated tooth, or a footprint impressed in once-wet mud. It is still possible to create a reliable portrait of unique, previously unknown creatures, but the accuracy of the art depends on the following:

- The quality and amount of actual skeletal material of the specimen preserved
- Discussion and collaboration with a paleontologist familiar with the fossil material and locality from which it was excavated
- Observation and comparisons to the closest related living forms
- The technical abilities, skill, and disciplined vision of the artist

The resulting artwork can draw the viewer back in time into exotic worlds of the ancient.

BATTLE SCARS— AN ARMORED DINOSAUR DEFENDS ITSELF

The armored dinosaur had spent the night sleeping under the broad branches of a huge fern plant on the edge of the forest. As the sun rose and began to warm the air, dew drops glistened on the fern fronds and other ground cover. A large dragonfly darted about. The ankylosaur stirred.

The bulky plant eater could have been mistaken for a huge mound of dirt and rocks in the darkness of night. He slept on his stomach, his four legs tucked beneath his body as best he could. His heavy armor plating, covering the top of his body from nose to tail, shielded him from the weather and helped him retain heat through the long nights.

A dragonfly landed on the tip of his nose. It tickled, making him stir. Although he opened his eyes to see what was disturbing his sleep, he was unable to look straight ahead because his eyes were only able to look to the sides. The dragonfly was in a blind spot directly in front of him. Shaking his head from side to side gave the dragonfly reason to find another place to perch. Now the ankylosaur was wide awake.

The ankylosaur was stiff from sleeping. His armor plating was heavy. He ambled up on all fours, shifting his enormous weight from leg to leg until he was standing firm. He left his hiding spot and emerged into an open field, shaking the stiffness from his bones.

This dinosaur was well protected by armor. It started on his head where small octagonal plates covered every inch of his skull. Each plate had a slightly rounded surface with a bony ridge or knob. The plates were larger over wide, flat areas of his skull and smaller around his eyes and the places that had to bend, like the back of his neck and the connections of his jaw. Even his eyes were covered by a protective bony shield.

Food was not far away. He could easily reach the kinds of plants that grew about three or four feet off the ground. He walked along the edge of the forest, nipping at ferns and cycads with his toothless, bony beak. His tongue was especially long and strong. He sometimes wrapped it around a low-hanging branch of a fern and pulled back with his head to strip the plant of fronds. His beak was wide and sharp. He often used it to snip off branches.

He was a slow and deliberate eater. The sun warmed his back as he moved quietly along, sampling the buffet of plentiful vegetation that marked the forest's edge. As he concentrated on eating, his long stiff tail wavered in the air, slowly bobbing with the weight of his bony tail club.

The forest was a terrific source of food for the armored dinosaur, but it was also a fine hiding place for meat eaters. Three dromaeosaurs, traveling as a small hunting pack, had their eyes on the ankylosaur. They slowly crept through the ferns, hidden in the dim forest light by the abundance of low-lying plants. Each dromaeosaur was about eight or nine feet long and sported sharp killing claws on its feet.

The noise of his munching and rustling through branches prevented the ankylosaur from hearing the approach of his attackers. Even so, just as the dromaeosaurs advanced to pounce on their prey, the ankylosaur picked up their scent and reacted more quickly than the meat eaters expected. The armored dinosaur turned quickly on his hind legs so that his rear end came around in the direction of the forest edge. With this turn, his deadly tail club swung around with great force in the direction of two of the attacking meat eaters. The first dromaeosaur was tripped by the middle part of the tail and fell to the ground. This was the lucky one. The second meat eater felt the full force of the tail club against its side. Its body was crushed like a rag doll being pounded with a sledgehammer. It was knocked against a nearby tree and died on the spot.

The third dromaeosaur had worked its way around the other side of the ankylosaur. As the armored dinosaur was busy fending off the other two attackers, the remaining dromaeosaur had

managed to leap onto the ankylosaur's back. It held tight with its feet and hand claws. The ankylosaur felt the weight of the attacker on his back and began to slowly run. The dromaeosaur held tightly with its hands and began to slash at the ankylosaur's neck with a foot claw. There was hardly a vulnerable spot to be found between the seams of the armor. Riding like a bronco cowboy, the dromaeosaur had very little time to do any damage. It was only going to be a matter of moments before the ankylosaur would

shake it loose. Of more concern to the meat eater were the sharp spikes that lined the back of the armored dinosaur's neck.

The ankylosaur lurched and shook to try to knock the dromaeosaur from its back. Finally, in one powerful flex of its spine, it whipped the attacker up and down on one of the neck spikes, puncturing the side of the dromaeosaur. The meat eater reeled in pain as it fell to the ground.

The injured dromaeosaur was unable to move for a moment

as it lay there gathering its senses. It would have been easy for the hulking ankylosaur to turn around and snuff out the life of the meat eater with one stomp of its leg. Instead, lacking the instinct of a killer and always wary of any meat eater, injured or not, the armored dinosaur headed away as fast as it could.

Soon, it would be munching at the forest edge again, this time hoping for a quiet meal without unexpected company.

Authors' Note—The preceding dinosaur story is fiction but is based on scientific evidence and ideas suggested by paleontologists. You will find explanations to support these ideas in the chapters that follow. Use the following guide to find some of these references:

- Eating habits and methods: page 79 (Feeding Habits and Adaptations)
- Armor plating: page 57 (Ankylosauria—Armored and Dangerous; Anatomy)
- Defensive behavior: page 86 (Armor, Clubs, Spikes, and Plates—The Decorations of Defense)
- Posture and locomotion: page 40 (Anatomy)
- Food: page 82 (What Did They Eat?)

CHAPTER 1

DINOSAURS DEFINED

What are dinosaurs? They were reptiles, but a special kind that no longer exists today. Many people assume that all dinosaurs were gigantic. Some confuse the dinosaurs with extinct reptiles that flew (the pterosaurs) and those reptiles that lived in the sea (e.g., plesiosaurs, ichthyosaurs, and mosasaurs). How does one know for sure whether a creature was a dinosaur or not?

Dinosaurs came in many shapes and sizes. Some were many times larger than the biggest land animals alive today. Others were as small as chickens. Some were carnivores that ate meat; others were herbivores that ate plants. Some dinosaurs walked on two legs, others on four legs. Yet, in spite of these vast differences, vertebrate paleontologists who study dinosaurs have identified many specific characteristics that allow them to classify dinosaurs as a group of related creatures, different from all others.

Dinosaurs lived only during the Mesozoic Era. The age of dinosaurs spanned from the Late Triassic Period about 225 million years ago to the end of the Late Cretaceous Period, some 65 million years ago. Fossils dating from before or after that time are not from dinosaurs. This rule also means that all dinosaurs are *extinct*, except for their modern relatives, the birds.

Dinosaurs were a special kind of reptile. Dinosaurs had basic characteristics common to all reptiles. They had a backbone and scaly skin, and they laid eggs. Meat-eating dinosaurs were also the ancestors of birds, with some showing birdlike features such as clawed feet, hollow bones, and even feathers.

Dinosaurs were land animals. Reptiles that flew in the air or lived in the water were around at the same time as dinosaurs, but they were *not* dinosaurs. Dinosaurs were built to walk and live on land only, although they may have occasionally waded in the water.

Dinosaurs had special skeletal features. Dinosaurs walked differently than other reptiles because of their hips. Dinosaurs had either ornithischian (birdlike) hips or saurischian (lizardlike) hips. Both kinds of hips allowed dinosaurs to walk with their legs tucked under their bodies to support their full weight. This mammal- or birdlike stance is clearly different from the sprawling stance of today's reptiles. A dinosaur would never have dragged its stomach along the ground like a crocodile or lizard. Other distinguishing skeletal features of dinosaurs included:

- Three or more vertebrae (backbones) attaching the spine to the hip.
- A ball-and-socket joint to attach the legs to the hip for increased mobility and flexibility.
- High ankles and long foot bones. (Dinosaurs walked on their toes.)
- A simple hinge joint at the ankle.
- Three or fewer finger bones on the fourth finger of each forefoot (hand) or no fourth finger at all.
- Three to five clawed or hoofed toes on the hind limb (foot).

Understanding Dinosaurs

The science of fossil organisms is called *paleontology. Paleo* means "ancient." Paleontologists use fossil traces of ancient organisms as a window onto life in the distant past, before the evolution of modern man.

Most of what we know about dinosaurs comes from our knowledge of their fossilized skeletons and the layers of earth in which they are found. Putting a dinosaur together is like doing a jigsaw puzzle without a picture to follow. Fortunately, because dinosaurs are vertebrates, all dinosaur skeletons are similar in some ways. A basic knowledge of vertebrate skeletons, and dinosaurs in particular, helps guide the paleontologist when putting together a new fossil jigsaw puzzle.

While no human being has ever seen a dinosaur in the flesh, much can be revealed by studying the fossil clues. The paleontologist must have a firm grasp of scientific methods and fact. He or she must also have a good imagination and a

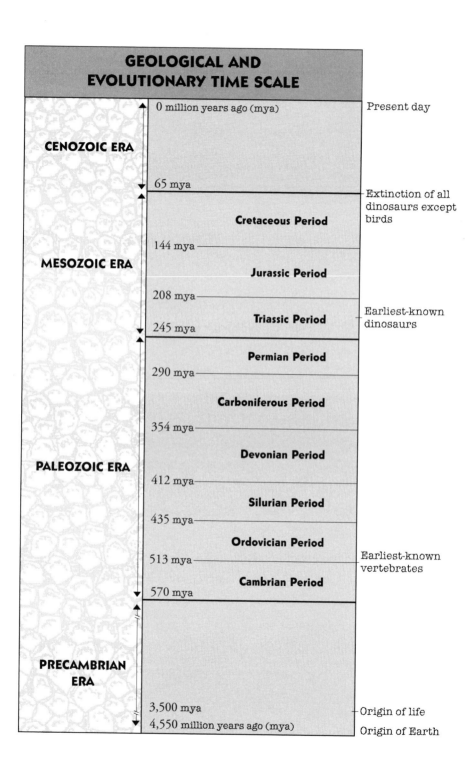

GEOLOGICAL AND EVOLUTIONARY TIME SCALE

CENOZOIC ERA

0 million years ago (mya) — Present day

65 mya — Extinction of all dinosaurs except birds

MESOZOIC ERA

Cretaceous Period

144 mya

Jurassic Period

208 mya

Triassic Period

245 mya — Earliest-known dinosaurs

PALEOZOIC ERA

Permian Period

290 mya

Carboniferous Period

354 mya

Devonian Period

412 mya

Silurian Period

435 mya

Ordovician Period

513 mya — Earliest-known vertebrates

Cambrian Period

570 mya

PRECAMBRIAN ERA

3,500 mya — Origin of life

4,550 million years ago (mya) — Origin of Earth

knack for solving mysteries. Fossils provide evidence for the construction of dinosaurs. The paleontologist examines these facts and tries to understand how they affected dinosaur lifestyle and behavior.

Our knowledge of dinosaurs grows every year. This book and others in this series will help you understand the many kinds of dinosaurs and how they lived. They are based on the latest scientific evidence and show us that dinosaur science is alive and well all over the world. After all, if scientific estimates are correct, there may have been as many as 1,200 unique kinds, or genera, of dinosaurs, only about 350 of which have been discovered.[1] If you decide to make a career out of dinosaur science, maybe one day you will add a new dinosaur or two to the list.

The Armored, Plated, and Bone-Headed Dinosaurs

Many of the most common plant-eating dinosaurs, including sauropods and ornithopods, were protected from predators by their size, speed, or ability to stay together in a herd. Many of the ceratopsian, or horned, dinosaurs had impressive horns to fend off their attackers. The plant-eating armored, plated, and bone-headed dinosaurs protected themselves differently. They relied on heavily armored bodies, tail clubs and spikes, or rock-hard skulls to discourage opposition.

The dinosaurs discussed in these pages were not closely related to each other and belonged to three distinct branches of the dinosaur family tree. The stegosaurs ("plated lizards") had large plates or spikes on their backs and a set of spikes at the ends of their tails. The ankylosaurs ("armored lizards") had extensive body armor. Some members of this group had large bony clubs at the ends of their tails. The pachycephalosaurs ("thick-headed lizards") had thick, bulbous skullcaps that could be used to headbutt opponents.

Armored, plated, and bone-headed dinosaurs have only slowly surfaced during the first 180 years of dinosaur science. The remains of these creatures are some of the rarest of all dinosaurs, but several excellent specimens provide clues to their nature.

In 1833, British doctor Gideon Mantell named *Hylaeosaurus* ("wood lizard"), the first armored dinosaur ever named. This was actually before the term *Dinosauria* itself had been coined. *Hylaeosaurus* was known at the time from a fragmentary skeleton that showed evidence of armor plating. Just what this creature looked like, however, would remain a mystery for many years until other armored dinosaurs were discovered. Two more famous members of the armored dinosaur family, *Nodosaurus* ("knobby lizard") and *Ankylosaurus* ("armored lizard"), were not discovered and described until 1889 and 1908, respectively. It was not until then that the truly astounding picture of these armor-shielded beasts was seen.

The first major discovery of a plated dinosaur was *Stegosaurus* ("plated lizard"), which lived during the Late Jurassic Period (about 150 million years ago) in North America alongside sauropods and large predators such as *Allosaurus*. It was discovered by a team of fossil collectors

Stegosaurus lived about 150 million years ago in northwestern North America alongside sauropods (*Brachiosaurus* pair, left) and large predators such as the meat-eating *Allosaurus* (distance).

working for the Yale Peabody Museum and professor Othniel C. Marsh. Several good specimens were recovered over the course of about ten years, but the dinosaur proved to be a tremendous puzzle to those who studied it. No previously discovered dinosaur had been found with back plates or tail spikes. The bones of the first specimens of this dinosaur were jumbled enough to make it impossible to know for certain where these parts belonged on the body. Fortunately for Marsh, a nearly complete specimen of *Stegosaurus* was found *in situ*—that is, with its bones lying in their natural positions to one another. From this specimen, Marsh was able to make a better guess at the arrangement of the back plates and knew with some certainty that the tail had four spikes.

The pachycephalosaurs, or bone-headed dinosaurs, were the last of these dinosaurs to be discovered. *Stegoceras* ("covered horn"), a small bipedal dinosaur only about six feet (two meters) long, was named in 1902, making it the first bone-headed dinosaur on record. Found in Alberta, Canada, its partial remains fooled its discoverer, Lawrence Lambe, into thinking he had discovered a horned dinosaur. He mistook the bony crown on top of its head for the base of a horn. It wasn't until 1924 that Charles W. Gilmore of the United States National Museum of Natural History was able to reveal the true nature of *Stegoceras*. He described a new specimen that included a complete skull and partial skeleton. The discovery of the skull of *Pachycephalosaurus* ("thick-headed lizard") in 1943 confirmed that there was more than one kind of bone-headed dinosaur. To this day, Gilmore's specimen of *Stegoceras* remains one of the most complete of any pachycephalosaur and makes it the best understood member of the family.

Armored and plated dinosaurs emerged during the Middle Jurassic Period in Asia, about 170 million years ago. The bone-headed dinosaurs were latecomers, not appearing in the fossil record until the middle part of the Early Cretaceous Period, about 120 years ago. The last of the stegosaurs appear to have died off about 100 million years ago, while the armored and bone-headed dinosaurs persisted until the end of the age of dinosaurs 65 million years ago.

Unlike some other plant-eating dinosaurs, the armored, plated, and bone-headed dinosaurs appear to have led a solitary existence. Their skeletons are found in isolation and rarely with others of their own kind. Whereas horned dinosaurs and duckbills appear to have traveled in large groups, there is no evidence to date that armored, plated, or bone-headed dinosaurs spent much time with one another.

The stegosaurs, ankylosaurs, and pachycephalosaurs evolved in roughly the following order:

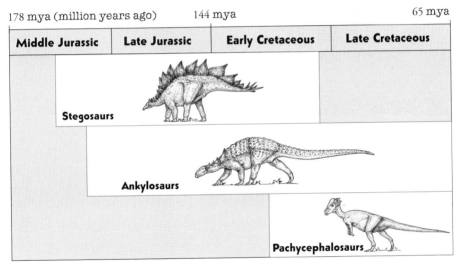

178 mya (million years ago)		144 mya		65 mya

Middle Jurassic	Late Jurassic	Early Cretaceous	Late Cretaceous

Stegosaurs

Ankylosaurs

Pachycephalosaurs

Armored, plated, and bone-headed dinosaurs make up only a small fraction of the dinosaurs currently known. Even when we combine their numbers, they account for only about 11 percent of all the individual kinds, or genera, of dinosaurs recognized so far. They may have been less plentiful than other plant eaters such as the sauropods, ornithopods, and ceratopsians, but they seem to have spread wide around the globe and to have survived a long, long time in their own way.

Chapter 2

Origins and Evolution

When the first dinosaurs evolved, they were part of a rich biological history of life on Earth that had already spanned hundreds of millions of years.

The earliest vertebrates all lived in the water. They included lampreys, sharks, and various other fish. About 370 million years ago, some ocean vertebrates adapted to breathing air and developed stronger limbs. This enabled them to leave the ocean and walk on land, at least for part of their lives. This was a monumental step in the evolution of the vertebrates.

Amphibians were some of the most successful early vertebrates to make the jump to land. But they were never able to completely separate themselves from their watery origins. Even today's amphibians begin as waterborne creatures and then take to the land as adults, returning to the water to lay and fertilize their eggs.

The most important biological event leading to true land animals was the evolution of the amniotes, vertebrate animals that could fertilize their eggs internally. This freed a creature from having to lay eggs in the water. We can thank the amphibians for being the evolutionary bridge to the first truly successful amniotes: the reptiles.

Reptiles were better suited for life on land for several reasons. Their eggs had firm or hard shells to protect them. Their limbs and other bones were sturdy enough to give them good mobility. Finally, their tough, scaly skin protected them from losing moisture. All these factors allowed reptiles to find great success on the land, and they evolved into many diverse families.

Today's amniotes include reptiles and birds, which lay shelled eggs, and mammals, whose fertilized eggs develop within their bodies. Humans, birds, lizards, snakes, turtles, and even dinosaurs are all related by being amniotes.

Dinosaurs fall within the group of vertebrates known as Reptilia, or reptiles. Reptiles are egg-laying backboned animals with scaly skin. The different kinds of reptiles, living and extinct, are grouped by certain features of their skeletons. Most important is the design of the reptilian skull. Dinosaurs fall within the subclass Diapsida, which included reptiles whose skulls had a pair of openings behind each eye. Diapsida is divided into two groups: the lepidosaurs and the archosaurs. Lepidosaurs consist of the kinds of lizards and snakes that live today. Archosaurs consist of the thecodonts, a group of reptiles from the Triassic Period; the crocodiles (living and extinct);

the pterosaurs (extinct flying reptiles); and the dinosaurs (extinct except for birds).[1] All dinosaurs are probably descendants of a single common archosaurian ancestor not yet identified.[2]

The dinosaurs and other diapsid reptiles were some of the most successful land vertebrates of all time. Dinosaurs first appeared about 225 million years ago and began to spread rapidly by the end of the Triassic Period.[3] Figure 1 summarizes the evolution of vertebrates leading to the dinosaurs and their bird descendents.

Dinosaur Beginnings

The earliest archosaurs were carnivores. Some evolved with four sprawling legs, while others gradually began to walk or sprint for short distances on their two hind legs. By the Late Triassic Period, about 225 million years ago, some two-legged, meat-eating creatures had evolved specialized hips and legs to help them stand erect. These hindquarters supported the full weight of their bodies while they walked on two feet. These animals, called thecodonts, ranged in size from about 6 inches (15 centimeters) to 13 feet (4 meters). They led to the first dinosaurs.

The earliest dinosaurs improved upon the design of their thecodont relatives in several ways. Their hips and limbs were better suited for standing upright on two legs; they did not sprawl like other reptiles. This freed their front legs and probably led to a more active lifestyle. With hands that were capable of grasping, they could pursue and hold on to prey in

Vertebrate Origins and Evolution
Leading to Dinosaurs

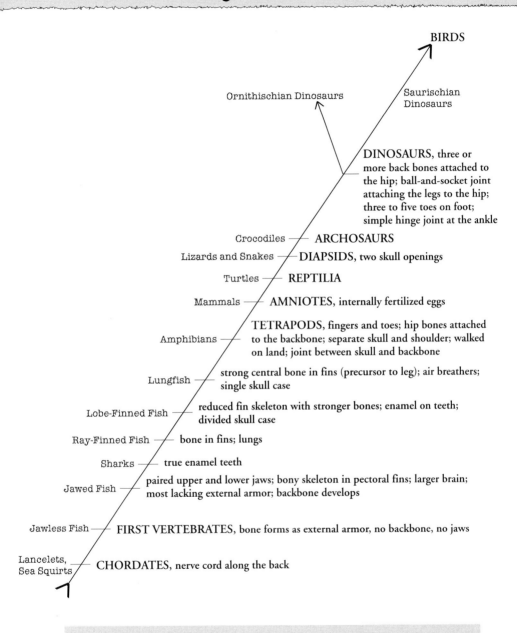

BIRDS

Ornithischian Dinosaurs

Saurischian Dinosaurs

DINOSAURS, three or more back bones attached to the hip; ball-and-socket joint attaching the legs to the hip; three to five toes on foot; simple hinge joint at the ankle

Crocodiles — ARCHOSAURS

Lizards and Snakes — DIAPSIDS, two skull openings

Turtles — REPTILIA

Mammals — AMNIOTES, internally fertilized eggs

Amphibians — TETRAPODS, fingers and toes; hip bones attached to the backbone; separate skull and shoulder; walked on land; joint between skull and backbone

Lungfish — strong central bone in fins (precursor to leg); air breathers; single skull case

Lobe-Finned Fish — reduced fin skeleton with stronger bones; enamel on teeth; divided skull case

Ray-Finned Fish — bone in fins; lungs

Sharks — true enamel teeth

Jawed Fish — paired upper and lower jaws; bony skeleton in pectoral fins; larger brain; most lacking external armor; backbone develops

Jawless Fish — FIRST VERTEBRATES, bone forms as external armor, no backbone, no jaws

Lancelets, Sea Squirts — CHORDATES, nerve cord along the back

Figure 1. This diagram shows how vertebrate animals evolved to yield dinosaurs. The steps along the way include evolutionary changes that are directly related to the traits of dinosaurs. The time span from the appearance of the first chordates to the last dinosaur is about 460 million years.

a way that their slower, less agile relatives could not. The early dinosaurs proved to have staying power.

By the Late Triassic Period, two distinct branches of dinosaurs had evolved based on their hip designs. The saurischians—those with lizardlike hips—included the meat-eating theropods and plant-eating prosauropods and sauropods. The ornithischians—those with birdlike hips—began as small two-legged ornithopod plant eaters in the Late Triassic Period. They eventually led to many plant-eating dinosaurs, including the armored, plated, and bone-headed dinosaurs, larger ornithopods (duckbills, iguanodonts, and others), and horned dinosaurs.

Armored, Plated, and Bone-Headed Dinosaur Groups

The armored, plated, and bone-headed dinosaurs were related to each other by being plant eaters with ornithischian hips. Otherwise, they were from different branches of the dinosaur family tree and not too much alike.

The armored and plated dinosaurs were bulky four-legged creatures that often measured about 20 to 30 feet (6 to 9 meters) in length, whereas the bone-headed dinosaurs were two-legged and measured between 6 and 15 feet (2.0 and 4.5 meters) long. They are grouped together in this book so that you may examine and compare their special adaptations for protection and how this affected their lives.

Of the dinosaurs included in this book, the plated dinosaurs, or stegosaurs, are thought to have been the first to appear. The earliest stegosaur fossils have been found in China and date from the Middle Jurassic Period, about 170 million years ago. They belong to a family of plated dinosaurs that is known by only one member, *Huayangosaurus* ("Huayang lizard"). It is viewed as being more primitive than the stegosaurs that appeared a little later, mostly in the Late Jurassic Period, based on characteristics of its skull and hips. The two families of stegosaurs are known as the Huayangosauridae and the Stegosauridae.

Armored dinosaurs are divided into two families depending on whether they had a tail club or not. Those with clubs are of the family Ankylosauridae, and those without are from the family Nodosauridae. The first known appearances of the Ankylosauridae were at the end of the Middle Jurassic Period and were followed in the Late Jurassic Period by the first known nodosaurs. Both families of armored dinosaurs outlasted the stegosaurs and were still around at the end of the Late Cretaceous Period when the last of the dinosaurs became extinct.

The bone-headed dinosaurs are from a dinosaur group called Pachycephalosauria. They were the latecomers of the dinosaurs included in this book. The first known member of the group, *Yaverlandia*, appeared in the Early Cretaceous Period. Most other known members of the bone-headed family are from the Late Cretaceous Period. Pachycephalosaurs are usually divided into two families based on the shape and slope of their skullcaps. Those with flatter heads are members of the family Homalocephalidae, and those with rounded, domed heads are members of the Pachycephalosauridae.

It is likely that the deepest roots of the armored and plated dinosaur family trees point to a common ancestor.[4] The most likely candidate is a four-legged ornithischian dinosaur named *Scelidosaurus* ("limb lizard") from the Early Jurassic which was found in England. *Scelidosaurus* had body armor in the form of small bony studs and its skull had similarities to both the stegosaurs and ankylosaurs that followed it later in the Jurassic Period.

A lack of early specimens makes the origins of the pachy-cephalosaurs murky, leaving paleontologists in the dark about which other dinosaurs might have been their closest relatives. There is growing agreement, however, that they may have been most closely related to the horned dinosaurs because of subtle similarities in the skulls of these two groups of dinosaurs. If this was the case, then the two groups probably

Scelidosaurus was probably the common ancestor of both the stegosaurs and ankylosaurs. It had body armor in the form of small bony studs.

split from a common ancestor and went on their separate evolutionary paths during the Late Jurassic Period.

The armored, plated, and bone-headed dinosaurs can be divided into distinct families based on common characteristics. The following two pages is a summary of the groups into which they fell, organized chronologically by known specimens.

Huayangosauridae ("Huayang lizards")

One of the two families of Stegosauria. Early stegosaurs and the most primitive of the Stegosauria. Known from only one member. Bulky four-legged plant eaters, highest at the hips, armored with two rows of small pointed back plates and four spikes on the tail. About 13 feet (4 meters) long. It had front teeth and cheek teeth. Found only in China.

Time: Middle Jurassic Period

Huayangosaurus

Stegosauridae ("roofed lizards")

One of the two families of Stegosauria. Bulky four-legged plant eaters, highest at the hips, armored with two rows of large pointed back plates and four spikes on the tail. Ranged in size from 10 to 30 feet (3 to 9 meters) long. Unlike the earlier huayangosaurs, members of this family had no front teeth; instead they used a toothless beak to snip plants that it chewed with cheek teeth. Found in North America, Europe, Africa, and Asia.

Time: Middle Jurassic to Early Cretaceous Periods

Chunkingosaurus,
Dacentrurus,
Kentrosaurus,
Lexovisaurus,
Tuojiangosaurus,
Wuerhosaurus

Stegosaurus

Ankylosauridae ("armored lizards")

One of the two families of Ankylosauria. Four-legged plant eaters with short necks, sturdy limbs, and heavily armored bodies. They had a bony tail club. The skull was broad and short with a toothless beak. They were the largest of the Ankylosauria, measuring from 18 to 27 feet (5.5 to 8 meters) long. Found in North America and Asia.

Time: Middle Jurassic to Late Cretaceous Periods

Ankylosaurus,
Gargoyleosaurus,
Nodocephalosaurus,
Pinacosaurus, Saichania,
Shamosaurus, Shanxia,
Talarurus,
Tarchia,
Tianchiasaurus,
Tianzhenosaurus,
Tsagantegia

Euoplocephalus

ARMORED, PLATED, AND BONE-HEADED DINOSAUR FAMILIES	SOME MEMBERS

Nodosauridae ("knobby lizards")

One of the two families of Ankylosauria. Four-legged plant eaters with short necks, sturdy limbs, and heavily armored bodies. They ranged in size from about 6 to 25 feet (2 to 7.5 meters) long, making their smallest members a little smaller than the ankylosaurids. They were heavily armored and spiked but did not have a bony tail club. The skull was narrow and long. With the exception of *Pawpawsaurus*, they had a toothless beak. Found in North America, Asia, Europe, and Australia.

Acanthopolis, Edmontonia, Hylaeosaurus, Minmi, Mymoorapelta, Nodosaurus, Panoplosaurus, Pawpawsaurus, Texasetes

Sauropelta

Time: Middle Jurassic to Late Cretaceous Periods

Homalocephalidae ("level heads")

One of the two families of the Pachycephalosauria. Two-legged plant eaters with a thick but flattened skullcap. They were small, ranging only from about 2 to 10 feet (0.6 to 3 meters) long. They had long legs, short arms, and a long stiff tail. They were probably good runners. They had small ridged teeth for shredding plants. Found in Asia.

Goyocephale, Wannanosaurus

Homalocephale

Time: Late Cretaceous Period

Pachycephalosauridae ("thick-headed lizards")

One of the two families of the Pachycephalosauria. Two-legged plant eaters with a thick, rounded skullcap. They were small to medium in size, ranging only from about 3 to 15 feet (0.9 to 4.5 meters) long. They had long legs, short arms, and a long stiff tail. They were probably good runners. They had small ridged teeth for shredding plants and are known mostly from skull material. Found in North America and Asia.

Micropachycephalosaurus, Prenocephale, Stegoceras, Stygimoloch, Tylocephale, Yaverlandia

Pachycephalosaurus

Time: Early to Late Cretaceous Periods

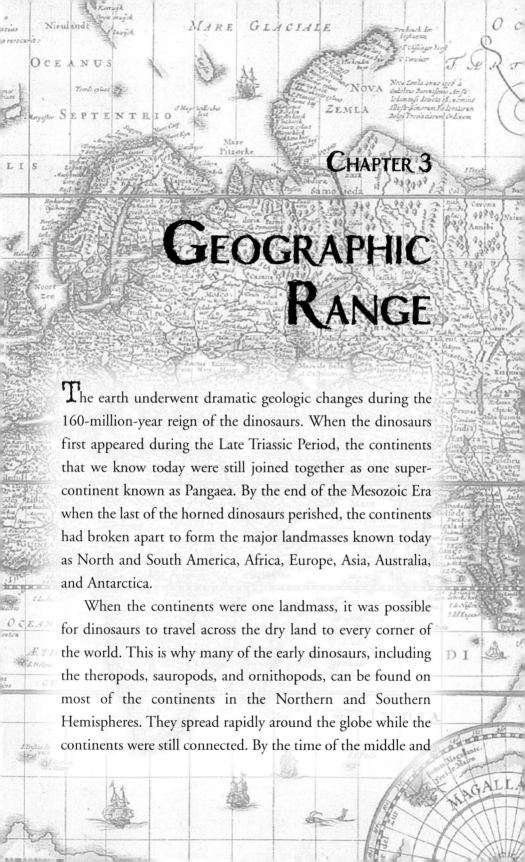

CHAPTER 3

GEOGRAPHIC RANGE

The earth underwent dramatic geologic changes during the 160-million-year reign of the dinosaurs. When the dinosaurs first appeared during the Late Triassic Period, the continents that we know today were still joined together as one super-continent known as Pangaea. By the end of the Mesozoic Era when the last of the horned dinosaurs perished, the continents had broken apart to form the major landmasses known today as North and South America, Africa, Europe, Asia, Australia, and Antarctica.

When the continents were one landmass, it was possible for dinosaurs to travel across the dry land to every corner of the world. This is why many of the early dinosaurs, including the theropods, sauropods, and ornithopods, can be found on most of the continents in the Northern and Southern Hemispheres. They spread rapidly around the globe while the continents were still connected. By the time of the middle and

TRIASSIC

EARLY JURASSIC

EARLY CRETACEOUS

later parts of the Cretaceous Period, when the first known pachycephalosaurs were appearing, the Northern and Southern Hemispheres had split apart. This made migration from the Northern Hemisphere to the Southern Hemisphere impossible. Today's arrangement of the continents was almost formed by the end of the Cretaceous Period, the end of the dinosaur era.

Armored, plated, and bone-headed dinosaurs appear to have originated in the Northern Hemisphere. The earliest ankylosaurs have been found in North America and the earliest stegosaurs have been found in China. The bone-headed dinosaurs have been found mostly in Asia and North America, except for the earliest one, *Yaverlandia*, named after the Yaverland Battery near where the specimen was found on the Isle of Wight in England. A few armored and plated dinosaurs have been found in the Southern Hemisphere, including Africa (stegosaurs) and Australia (nodosaur). North America was still connected to Asia by a land bridge during the earlier part of the Late Cretaceous Period. This accounts for the similarities between the armored, plated, and bone-headed dinosaurs found on these two continents.

Range of Stegosaur, and Fossil Locations

- Ankylosauria
- Stegosauria
- Pachycephalosauria

Ankylosaur, Pachycephalosaur Around the World

CHAPTER 4

ANATOMY

All organisms are made up of biological systems, such as the skeletal and muscular systems. The study of these structures is called anatomy. Studying the anatomy of an organism is different from studying how the structures are *used* in the organism. The study of how the body works, physiology, is covered in the next chapter.

Dinosaurs Are Vertebrates

Dinosaurs are part of the lineage of animals known as vertebrates—animals with backbones. The first vertebrates were fish, followed by amphibians, reptiles, dinosaurs, and mammals and birds. To the best of our knowledge, the first vertebrate ancestors appeared about 520 million years ago in the form of jawless fish.[1] Dinosaurs first walked the earth about 225 million years ago, nearly 300 million years after fish had begun to populate the oceans.

Regardless of whether they live in the water, walk the land, or fly in the air, all vertebrates share some common characteristics. The most basic common feature of the vertebrate body is that one side of the body is a mirror image of the other. This principle is called bilateral symmetry. A second common feature is that the organs of vertebrates have descended from what were basically the same organs in their ancestors. This idea is called the principle of homology.

Dinosaurs shared many similar skeletal features with other vertebrates, living and extinct. Even though we rarely, if ever, see the fossil remains of soft tissue or organs of the dinosaurs—such as the brain, lungs, liver, and gut—we can assume that they shared many of the internal organs of today's land-dwelling vertebrates. These ideas allow scientists to understand what a living dinosaur was really like.

The Dinosaur Hip

All dinosaurs are divided into two large groups based on the structure of their hipbones. The saurischian ("lizard-hipped") group is comprised of the two-legged carnivorous theropods; the four-legged, long-necked herbivorous sauropods; and the two-legged herbivorous prosauropods. The ornithischian ("bird-hipped") group includes all others, such as the armored, horned, and duck-billed dinosaurs.

Both kinds of dinosaur hips allowed the hind legs to be attached underneath the body so that they could bear the entire weight of the creature. The hind legs were also connected to the hip with a ball-and-socket joint. This provided dinosaurs with increased flexibility and mobility over their reptile ancestors. The front legs were also positioned underneath the body to help bear the weight of those dinosaurs that walked on all fours.

The legs of the modern reptile, such as a crocodile or lizard, are attached to the sides of its body and do not support the full weight of the body while the creature is at rest. Reptiles lay their bellies on the ground and rise up only when they need to move. On the other hand, the position of a dinosaur was "always up." Dinosaurs probably had a more energetic metabolism than today's reptiles simply because it required more stamina to hold up their body weight.

Dinosaur legs were designed more like those of mammals or birds but with some clear distinctions. While the joints in their shoulders and hips were flexible in several directions, those in the knees and elbows could only move in one direction.

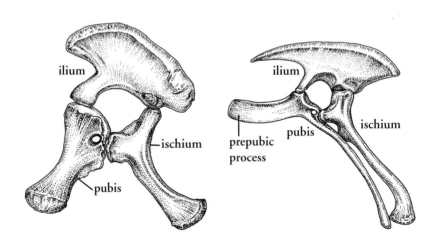

There are two kinds of dinosaur hips: saurischian ("lizard-hipped," left) and ornithischian ("bird-hipped," right).

This, combined with an ankle that was more like a door hinge than a ball and socket, restricted the bending of a dinosaur's forelimbs and hind limbs in one plane of motion, forward or backward. Unlike humans and other mammals, which can move sideways with ease, a dinosaur had to turn its body if it wanted to move to the side. Dinosaurs would have made lousy soccer goalies.

The armored, plated, and bone-headed dinosaurs all had ornithischian hips. The stegosaurs and ankylosaurs walked on four legs and the pachycephalosaurs walked on two.

Bodies of the Armored, Plated, and Bone-Headed Dinosaurs

Some of the armored, plated, and bone-headed dinosaurs were among the rarest of all dinosaurs. Although diverse in their characteristics, several members of these families are represented by only a few specimens. Only twelve kinds of stegosaurs are known, and seven of these are represented by only partial skeletons. Furthermore, new kinds of stegosaurs are not found very often. The most recently discovered member of this group was found in 1983 (*Chungkingosaurus*).

Of the twelve recognized species of pachycephalosaurs, eight are known only from skulls and skull fragments. The last time a new species of bone-headed dinosaur was named was 1983 (*Stygimoloch*).

In contrast to the stegosaurs and pachycephalosaurs, ankylosaurs have recently been the beneficiary of a boom in discoveries. Armored dinosaurs are now represented by twenty-six genera, or kinds.

Fortunately for us, even the rarest of these groups of dinosaurs is represented by several spectacular specimens. They are surely some of the strangest and awe-inspiring creatures ever to have rumbled across the earth.

Stegosauria–The Plated Dinosaurs

The Stegosauria consisted of medium- to large-sized plant eaters measuring in length from 10 to 30 feet (3 to 9 meters). They are distinguished from other dinosaurs by their skull design, tail weaponry, and back plates. The two families of Stegosauria—the huayangosaurs and the stegosaurs—had the following features:

- They had ornithischian hips and walked on four legs.
- The body was highest at the hips, although somewhat less so in the primitive *Huayangosaurus*. This was due to having short front legs and long back legs.
- Some had shoulder spikes.
- They had two rows of plates or spikes running from the base of the neck down the back to the tail. These varied in size and were largest over the back and hip region. In *Stegosaurus*, they consisted of seventeen thin, upright plates, no two of the same exact shape or size. These were positioned in two alternating rows along the back of the animal. Other stegosaurs had similar arrangements of the back plates, although they were usually smaller and found in different numbers than in *Stegosaurus*. The plates themselves were thin, bony, and inflexible. They were firmly

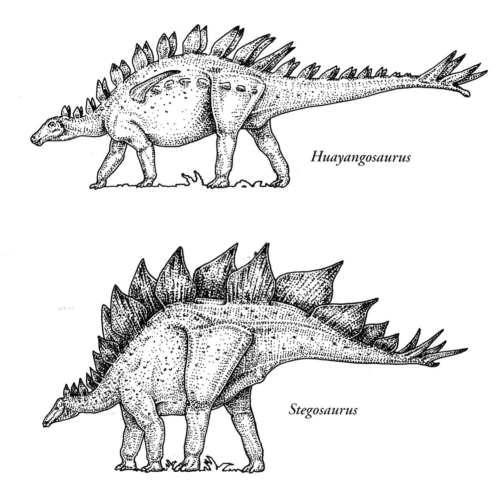

Huayangosaurus

Stegosaurus

The two families of Stegosauria are represented by *Huayangosaurus* and *Stegosaurus*.

attached to the skin and could probably have been wiggled by skin muscles.

- Their tails had two pairs of defensive spikes pointing out to the sides.

- Their skulls were long, short, and narrow in stegosaurs but somewhat taller and wider in *Huayangosaurus*.

- The stegosaurs had a toothless beak and small, triangular, ridged teeth in the cheek area. The huayangosaurs had seven teeth in the upper front part of the jaw in addition to the typical cheek teeth.

- Unlike most other ornithischians, the Stegosauria did not have tails that were stiffened by bony tendons. Since a stiffened tail enabled other dinosaurs to keep better balance when they ran, it could be presumed that the Stegosauria were not speed demons. This idea is supported by the stocky and inflexible design of their limbs and feet. The Stegosauria probably moved with the stiffened pace of an elephant.[2]

- In addition to the back plates and spikes, stegosaurs also had some minor armor plating in the form of small bony nodes protecting the throat.

Ankylosaurs–The Armored Dinosaurs

The Ankylosauria consisted of medium- to large-sized plant eaters measuring in length from about 6 to 27 feet (1.8 to 8 meters). They are distinguished from other dinosaurs by having extensive body armor. The two families of Ankylosauria—the nodosaurs and the ankylosaurs—had the following features:

- Their skulls were wide and triangular when viewed from above. Armor plates were fused to the skull.

Ankylosaur skulls were shorter than those of nodosaurs.

- Ankylosaurs had a stiffened tail with a bony club on the end, which was undoubtedly used for protection against predators. Nodosaurs did not have a stiffened tail or club.

- Ankylosaurs and nodosaurs were covered with extensive body armor as well as a number of bony knobs and spikes. The armor came in several sizes of oval and rectangular plates distributed like a mosaic over most

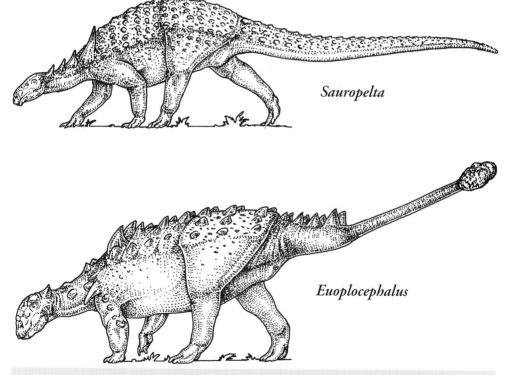

Sauropelta

Euoplocephalus

The armored dinosaurs consisted of two families, the nodosaurs (without a tail club) and the ankylosaurs (with a tail club). Shown here are the nodosaur *Sauropelta* and the ankylosaur *Euoplocephalus*.

of the animal's body. The neck and shoulders were typically covered by curving bands of rectangular plates. The plates themselves consisted of hard bone, and the gaps between the plates were often filled with small bony ossicles. The belly was sometimes protected by these small bony beads as well.

- Their teeth were triangular and had ridges, much like those of stegosaurs. They were deeply set into the cheek area.

- The snout and skull of the most advanced ankylosaurs had a complex network of air chambers through which the armored dinosaurs breathed. This may have improved their sense of smell and possibly acted as a resonating chamber for making sounds.[3]

- Ankylosaurs and nodosaurs were tallest at the hips. Their stocky legs were adapted for carrying their heavy weight. The limbs of nodosaurs were a little lighter than those of ankylosaurs, but both families were slow-moving and probably not as fast as the horned dinosaurs or ornithopods.[4]

Pachycephalosaurs–The Bone-Headed Dinosaurs

The Pachycephalosauria consisted of small- to medium-sized bipedal plant eaters measuring in length from about 2 to 15 feet (0.6 to 4.5 meters). They are the only dinosaur group distinguished by a thick, bony skullcap. They had the following features:

- A thick, bony skullcap. The pachycephalosaurids were the larger variety and had a rounded skullcap. Homalocephalids were generally smaller and had a thickened but flattened skullcap.

Homalocephale

Pachycephalosaurus

The Pachycephalosauria included two families. The homalocephalids were smaller and had a thickened but flattened skull cap, illustrated in *Homalocephale* (top). The pachycephalosaurids had a rounded skull cap, as seen in *Pachycephalosaurus* (below).

- In addition to their thick bony caps, the skulls of the Pachycephalosauria were ornamented in several unusual ways. *Stegoceras* had a sharp ridge with bony knobs and spikes forming a circle around the midline of the skull. *Homalocephale* ("level head") had a flat head with bony knobs on top and small horns pointing to the rear over the neck. *Stygimoloch* ("Hell Creek demon") had a bit of everything—rounded skullcap, bony spikes on its nose, a protective row of bony knobs over the eyes, and a pair of formidable spikes jutting up from behind the ears.

- They had a heavy, stiffened tail to aid in balance. Although, they walked on two feet, they leaned so that their back was level to the ground.

- Their backbones were designed with a ridge-in-groove structure that enabled them to lock effectively and hold the back straight. This probably helped absorb the shock of head butting, safeguarding the skull and brain from excessive jarring.

- They had small spatula-shaped teeth set in the cheek area as well as several conical canine teeth in the front portion of the upper jaw. Pachycephalosauria were presumably plant eaters, although they may have also eaten insects.

- The arms, or forelimbs, were short compared to the hind limbs.

- The upper part of the leg—the femur—was longer than the lower part—the tibia. This suggests that they were not fast runners. However, their legs were strong and sturdy.

It seems obvious that the armor plating, spikes, and bony tail clubs of plated and armored dinosaurs were used to protect them from large meat-eating predators such as *Allosaurus* and *Ceratosaurus* that lived during their time. But what about the bony skullcaps of the Pachycephalosauria? Did they protect themselves by butting against the belly of their attackers? Probably not.

Some scientists believe that the crash-helmet skulls of the bone-headed dinosaurs were used by rival males during head-butting contests over mates. The same kind of behavior can be seen today in bighorn sheep. They square off and repeatedly butt heads with all their might until one male is forced to give

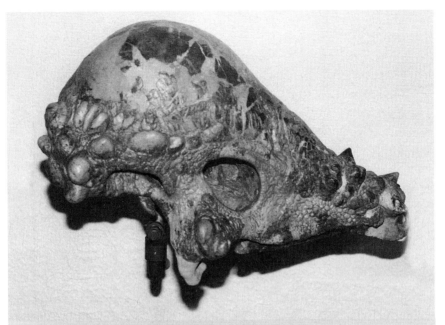

The skull cap of *Pachycephalosaurus* was thick and bony. *Pachycephalosaurus* is the largest known bone-headed dinosaur. Its skull measured about 2 feet (0.6 meters) in length. Its whole body may have been about 15 feet (4.5 meters) long.

up and back off. Pachycephalosaurs may have done the same, squaring off with their battering-ram skulls, running headlong into each other. However, since the skullcap of these dinosaurs was rounded and small, some scientists now doubt whether head butting was common among pachycephalosaurs. They would have had to have great aim to make it work. Otherwise, their heads would have just glanced off each other. Instead, these dinosaurs may have used their heads to ram against the side of a rival in the rib area, a contest that might have been a little less jarring to the brain.[5] Imagine getting a charley horse from a bowling ball striking your thigh, and you'll have an idea what this might have felt like.

The backbones of pachycephalosaurs were especially designed to absorb the shock of such contests, and their legs were strong enough to propel them forward with astonishing power. Their shock-absorber necks allowed them to engage in head- and thigh-banging contests with little danger of permanent injury. The various knobs and spikes adorning their skulls were probably also important ways to tell one individual from another, and to display one's prowess to members of the opposite sex.

Armored, Plated, and Bone-Headed Dinosaur Skulls

The skulls of the armored, plated, and bone-headed dinosaurs were different in many ways. The skulls of the Stegosauria were some of the smallest for dinosaurs of their size. The heavily armored skulls of the Ankylosauria provided ample protection for the eyes, the top of the head, and neck. The Pachycephalosauria were built with crash-test helmets for skulls and shock absorbers for necks.

Dinosaur Skin, Armor Plating, and Fancy Backs

Dinosaur skin, like other soft body parts of these animals, was almost never fossilized. The skin of dinosaurs easily decomposed and disappeared long before fossilization could take place. Although there is some evidence about dinosaur skin, it is

Stegosaurus (plated dinosaur)

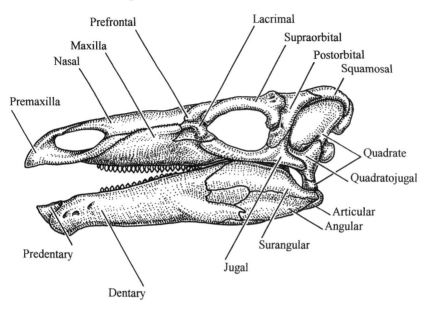

Prefrontal

Lacrimal

Supraorbital

Maxilla

Postorbital

Nasal

Squamosal

Premaxilla

Quadrate

Quadratojugal

Articular

Angular

Surangular

Predentary

Jugal

Dentary

Euoplocephalus
(armored dinosaur)

Stegoceras
(bone-headed dinosaur)

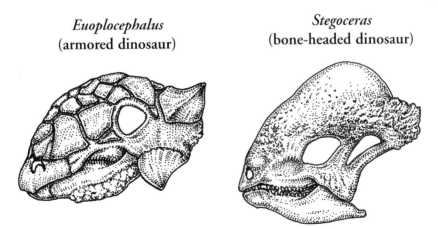

These illustrations show the unique skulls of the plated, armored, and bone-headed dinosaurs.

extremely rare. When evidence of dinosaur skin does exist, as it does for several duck-billed dinosaurs, it shows that they had nonoverlapping scales similar to those of the modern monitor lizard. These scales varied in size across different parts of the body. They were generally smaller, for flexibility, around the head and joints such as the neck and knees and larger along broad parts of the body and tail.

A fossilized skin impression is *not* the dinosaur skin itself, but the pattern of the skin that was left behind in the mud or sand where a dinosaur died. Skin impressions are known as trace fossils. They represent a trace of the dinosaur that made them, rather than the fossilized parts of the dinosaur itself.

In the case of armored and plated dinosaurs, what is normally thought of as skin was often covered or replaced by an extensive array of armor plating, plates, spikes, and spines. These armored coverings were more durable than normal skin and have been exquisitely preserved in the fossil record in several spectacular cases.

Stegosaurs—Bony Beads and Plates

In addition to the spectacular bony plates and spikes that adorned their backs and tails, the skin of the stegosaurs sometimes had additional armored protection. The throat was dotted with small bony knobs called ossicles. The ossicles were tightly packed like the chain mail in a suit of armor to protect the throat area. At least one other stegosaur, *Huayangosaurus*, had additional armor in the form of several bony plates on its sides.

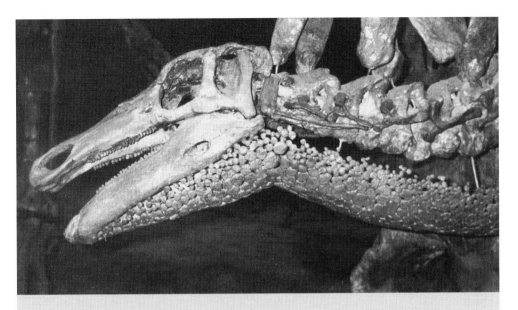

The throat of *Stegosaurus* was protected by a coat of small bony nodes.

The back plates of stegosaurs varied in size and shape from the large triangular forms of *Stegosaurus* to the smaller pointed plates and spikes found in *Kentrosaurus* and *Huayangosaurus*. The plates were not attached to the spine, but were embedded in the thick skin of the neck, back, and tail. In nearly all but *Stegosaurus*, the plates were positioned in pairs running along the backbone. *Stegosaurus* had seventeen large plates running in a staggered or alternating pattern along the neck, back, and tail. The tail of all stegosaurs ended with a pair of prickly spikes.

The purpose of the back plates is not entirely understood. Originally thought to provide protection, at least one early view was that the plates lay flat on the back like shingles on a roof. Close examination of the structure of the plates reveals, however, that they were not rock solid in real life but rich with blood vessels.

As a means of protection, the plates would have been no match for the bone-crunching teeth of a large predatory dinosaur. However, the plates were visually stunning and could have served to make the animal appear larger and more threatening. As a means of display, and while perhaps showing

Stegosaurus had seventeen large plates in two staggered rows along its neck, back, and tail. The plates were not attached to the spine, but were embedded in the thick skin.

distinctive color patterns, the plates could have played a role in distinguishing one individual from another. This would have been a useful feature when vying for a mate. It is even possible that the rich blood supply in the plates allowed the dinosaurs to change the color of their plates at will, much like a chameleon does today.[6] This would have been a handy calling card during mating season.

In addition to their use for visual display, it is thought that the plates were probably excellent conductors of heat. The flow of blood that permeated the plates would have made them an effective heat exchange system. Heat would have been dissipated from the plates during hot weather and gathered for absorption by the dinosaur in cool weather.[7]

Ankylosauria–Armored and Dangerous

The ankylosaurids and nodosaurids are unique in the annals of dinosaur history. No other family of dinosaurs was as extensively protected by armor plating as these creatures. As a result, they were probably somewhat slow-moving and relied on their armor as their main form of protection against predators.

The armor plating of these creatures had many special characteristics:[8]

- Head armor formed a mosaic of thick, bony plates that were actually fused to the skull. The head was completely covered on its top surface, including bony studs around the eyes. One kind, *Euoplocephalus*, even had a bony eyelid.

- Armor consisted of small spines, bony knobs, long spikes, and flat and rounded plates of various sizes.

- The plates of ankylosaurs and nodosaurs were normally arranged in stripes or bands along the neck, back, and tail. Some of it was embellished by knobs and spines, especially on the back. Flat or pointed bony plates are called scutes. The space between the scutes was filled with a matrix of smaller scutes or bony ossicles.[9] The nodosaur *Edmontonia* had several bands of very large plates crossing the back from side to side. The largest plates were over the shoulders and were six- or eight-sided with a sharp ridge down the center. The back armor of another nodosaur, *Sauropelta*, consisted of smaller knobby plates than those of *Edmontonia*, but they were thicker and had a point or

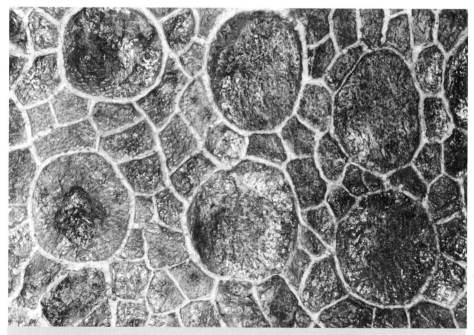

The back armor of *Sauropelta* consisted of small knobby plates that had a point or ridge. They fit together like a mosaic of tiles to provide protection from attacking predators.

ridge. The armored dinosaur for which there is the most evidence is *Euoplocephalus*, an ankylosaur from Montana and Alberta, Canada. The topside of this animal was completely protected by a bony mosaic of scutes from the tip of its nose to the bony tail club.

- Large spikes often protruded from the sides of the armored dinosaurs, mostly in the region of the front limbs and head. The shoulders, neck, and back were often well protected by these spines.

The ankylosaurs had a bony club at the end of their tails; the nodosaurs did not. The tail could have been swung with great force to injure or even break the leg of an attacking predator.

Pachycephalosaurs–Prehistoric Crash-Test Dummies

The skeletons of bone-headed dinosaurs are extremely rare. Most are known mainly from their skulls. Nothing is known about pachycephalosaur skin patterns. Although their skulls were sometimes adorned with a crown of spikes or knobs, it is unknown at the present time if their skin was armored or plated.

CHAPTER 5

PHYSIOLOGY

Physiology is the study of how a body operates. The physiology of dinosaurs is understood by comparing the evidence from fossils to the anatomy and physiology of today's creatures. Other physical evidence, such as trackways, has also been used to piece together what we know about the behavior and movement of dinosaurs.

Brains and Smarts–A Look at the Dumb and Dumber Dinosaurs

On the scale of intelligence, the armored and plated dinosaurs ranked among the dimmest of dinosaurs. To understand how this can be known, one needs to understand how the size of the brain can be used to measure an animal's smarts.

Determining the intelligence of dinosaurs is a task that can, essentially, never be proven. After all, what *is* intelligence? Intelligence can be described as the ability to process information, or to learn. Since this is something we will never be able to observe in dinosaurs, we must rely on other clues to intelligence that are found in the fossil record. Chief among these is the size of the dinosaur's brain in proportion to the size of its body.

In examining many kinds of living animals, scientists have found a relationship between the size of the brain and the size of a creature's body. A species whose brain is larger than expected for its body size is considered more intelligent. This allows one to compare the intelligence of animals of different body sizes, say a Pekingese dog with an Irish wolfhound. By this measure, mammals and birds are considered to be more intelligent than fish, amphibians, and reptiles. What makes humans so unusual is that our brain size is seven times greater than should be expected for a creature with our body size.

The brain, like other soft tissues and organs, is not preserved in the fossil record. However, the approximate size of a dinosaur's brain can be determined by measuring and casting the cavity in the skull where the brain once was. The cavity is called the braincase. Unfortunately, most dinosaur skull material is too incomplete to include the braincase. Even when the braincase is present, this space is not often well preserved due to the compression and crushing of the skull during fossilization. Measurements have thus far been made for less than 5 percent of all known dinosaurs, so much work remains in this area.[1]

Braincases have been preserved for several members of the armored, plated, and bone-headed dinosaurs. Their brain-size to body-size ratio was not impressive. On average, the brain power of these dinosaurs was comparable to that of a modern crocodile. It would appear that the Ankylosauria were the dumbest of this group, followed by the tiny-headed Stegosauria. However, both were probably a little brighter than the sauropods (long-necked plant eaters). The Pachycephalosauria, while no geniuses in the dinosaur kingdom, were probably a little smarter than the armored and plated dinosaurs, but not by much.[2] What they all lacked in smarts, though, they seemed to possess in defensive armor and brute strength. None of these creatures would have made easy pickings for one of the larger theropods of the time.

A word should be said here about that misunderstood mental marvel, *Stegosaurus.* When fabled paleontologist Othniel C. Marsh first discussed the brain of this unusual creature, he noticed that in addition to a small braincase, the rear section of the spine contained a "very large chamber . . . formed by an enlargement of the spinal canal." He noted that this "suggestive subject" might lead one to believe that the creature had an auxiliary brain in its rear end, an idea that quickly caught the public's attention. One journalist was even moved to publish the following poem casting humor upon the poor stegosaur:[3]

> Behold the mighty Dinosaur,
> Famous in prehistoric lore
> Not only for his weight and length
> But for his intellectual strength.
> You will observe by these remains
> The creature had two set of brains,
> One in his head (the usual place),
> The other at his spinal base.
> Thus he could reason a priori

As well as a posteriori.
No problem bothered him a bit,
He made both head and tail of it.
So wise he was; so wise and solemn,
Each thought filled just a spinal column.
If one brain found the pressure strong,
It passed a few ideas along.
If something slipped his forward mind
'Twas rescued by the one behind.
And if in error he was caught,
He had a saving afterthought.
As he thought twice before he spoke,
He had no judgment to revoke.
For he could think without congestion
Upon both sides of every question.
O! Gaze upon this model beast,
Defunct ten thousand years,* at least.

—Bert L. Taylor
Chicago Tribune, 1927

Authors' note: We rush to remind the reader that Taylor's estimate of "ten thousand years, at least" is off by about 150 million years!

The dinosaur with two brains—one for its front and one for its rear—turned out to be a fiction. The cavity in its backbone was no more than a widening in the nerve canal. The same kind of cavity has since been observed in sauropods, birds, and many land vertebrates. In birds, the extra space is taken up by a structure known as a glycogen body. The glycogen body appears to supply a reserve of carbohydrates to the nervous system to help nerve fibers grow. Perhaps dinosaurs such as *Stegosaurus* had this in common with birds.[4]

Senses

Herbivorous creatures rely on their senses to locate food and avoid danger. A good sense of smell might pick up the scent of a stalking predator or a grove of tasty vegetation over the next hill. A good sense of hearing, like smell, provides clues to the presence of carnivores before they can be seen. Keen eyesight is important for finding food and noticing the movements of an approaching meat eater.

Evidence for these senses can be seen by studying the braincase and other parts of a dinosaur's skull.

The braincase in a dinosaur skull holds clues to the many connections between the brain and other parts of the body. Evidence of these nerve connections can be seen in the form of holes in the braincase through which nerves were once threaded to attach the brain to other organs.

The brains of modern vertebrates—particularly reptiles and birds—are similar in many ways. The sense of smell is located at the front of the brain in the olfactory lobe, and vision is concentrated in an optic lobe near the center. Observing the kinds of nerve connections that exist in today's animals can help a paleontologist identify the locations of similar features in dinosaur skulls.

Braincases that have been studied for the Stegosauria and Ankylosauria show that these animals' senses were average and unremarkable. They were undoubtedly slow-witted and slow-moving creatures. When attacked, they probably relied most heavily on their body armor and defensive weapons for protection. The Pachycephalosauria, however, were somewhat more advanced in the brain department.

The brain of the Pachycephalosauria possessed enlarged olfactory lobes—the part of the brain used for sensing smell. These dinosaurs probably had an excellent sense of smell. This was important to survival because its primary means of defense was to run away. If a bone head could smell a predator coming from a distance, it would have an extra margin of time in which to flee.

The eyes of the pachycephalosaurs were also directed somewhat toward the front, providing them with slightly overlapping fields of vision. This provided better depth perception for viewing predators, but was also necessary for clearly seeing and maneuvering itself during head-butting contests with others of its kind.

Growth Rate

Newly hatched dinosaurs were small, yet they sometimes grew to enormous sizes that were often thousands of times their original weight. What can the fossil record tell us about how fast the dinosaurs grew from hatchling to adult?

To understand how fast dinosaurs grew, scientists need to have three things. The first is a keen knowledge of how fast modern reptiles, birds, and other animals grow. Then scientists can keep their guesses about dinosaurs in perspective. Information about reptile growth is abundant. Also, reptiles continue to grow throughout their lives, unlike birds and mammals that reach a peak size soon after reaching sexual maturity. Many scientists believe that the dinosaurs had a growth pattern similar to reptiles. This is one reason that we continue to discover larger and larger specimens of the same kind of dinosaur, such as *Tyrannosaurus*. Each larger specimen may simply represent an individual that was

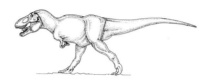

Tyrannosaurus

older than others, and therefore continued to grow for a longer time.

The second thing needed to understand the growth rates of dinosaurs is a series of fossil skeletons for a given kind of dinosaur that represents several life stages. This is available in abundance for some dinosaurs, but unfortunately not for any of the armored, plated, or bone-headed dinosaurs.

The third thing needed to understand how fast dinosaurs grew is a way in which to connect what is seen in the bones to the growth span of the dinosaur. One attempt to do this has come in the form of microscopic studies of dinosaur bone. A magnified cross section of bone reveals clues about dinosaur growth.

At one extreme, some bones formed in a smooth, continuous pattern. This indicates that the dinosaur was growing continuously and steadily. At the other extreme, some bone tissue formed with curious rings called lines of arrested growth. These growth rings are much like the seasonal rings in cross sections of tree trunks. This phenomenon is also seen in the bones of modern reptiles. It represents an annual period when growth slows down, perhaps during a cool season when the animal is less active for an extended period.

There are few specimens of young armored, plated, and bone-headed dinosaurs. The closest thing to a growth series that exists for these dinosaurs is for the ankylosaur *Pinacosaurus* ("board lizard"), but even this series is considered incomplete because it lacks truly young members such as babies and "toddlers." Without a complete growth series to examine, it is difficult to know how long it took for these dinosaurs to reach adult size. Paleontologist Robert Bakker has examined some of the isolated bones of a young stegosaur. He believes the microscopic bone structure indicates that the animal grew rapidly, attaining its adult weight of about five tons in six years.[5] While most paleontologists would rather wait until there is better evidence to explain the growth rate of these dinosaurs, one might speculate that a dinosaur the size of *Stegosaurus* or *Euoplocephalus* may have grown at a rate comparable to other dinosaurs for which there is better evidence.

There is an abundance of evidence for several ornithopods (two-footed, plant-eating dinosaurs) that they grew rapidly for several years before slowing down when they reached adulthood. What is most surprising is just how fast they grew. The duck-billed dinosaur *Maiasaura* from Montana required only about seven years to reach its maximum size of 30 feet (9 meters).[6] During its first few years of growth, it did not show evidence of growth rings, suggesting that it grew continuously without seasonal interruptions.[7] *Maiasaura* reached adult size about twice as fast as crocodiles and humans.[8] Growing up fast would have been important because these dinosaurs were defenseless against predators until they were large enough to use their size for protection. The same might not have been so important to the survival of armored or plated dinosaurs, which relied on armor plating and defensive weaponry to fend off attackers. It is unlikely that they had the same elevated growth rates as *Maiasaura*.

A more conservative estimate would be that the armored and plated dinosaurs grew at a rate comparable to that of horned dinosaurs. One study of *Protoceratops*, for which there is an abundance of specimens representing a growth cycle, estimates that they required between twelve and twenty-three years to reach maturity.[9]

Aside from how fast the dinosaurs grew, can paleontologists tell how long an individual may have lived? This question is also tricky. A dinosaur could have lived many more years after any significant growth. Best guesses for the life span of dinosaurs come from observing modern-day animals with similar sizes and metabolisms. It is possible that the smaller bone-headed dinosaurs lived between fifteen and twenty years, and that the larger armored and plated dinosaurs lived for more than fifty.

Were Dinosaurs Warm-Blooded?

Scientists think that dinosaurs were not the slow and sluggish creatures that they once thought them to be. Dinosaurs were built for action and could probably have moved quite fast when needed. Some dinosaurs also grew rapidly, outpacing the rate of growth often seen in modern mammals. But not all dinosaurs were alike in this way. Some grew quite slowly, and there were many others in between.

Does this tell us whether dinosaurs were endotherms (warm-blooded) or ectotherms (cold-blooded)? This is a question that many paleontologists have argued. Unfortunately, there is no simple answer or single piece of fossil evidence that can tell us for sure.

There are two factors that determine whether an animal is warm- or cold-blooded. One is the source of heat. Was it internal, as in endotherms, or external, as in ectotherms? The other factor is the consistency of body temperature. Was it constant or variable?

If we look at today's animals, we can see that small and large mammals are warm-blooded and that reptiles of all sizes are cold-blooded. Dinosaurs were reptiles, so they were originally thought to be cold-blooded. However, current thinking shows that dinosaurs were highly active and unique kinds of creatures, clearly different from other reptiles in many ways. How could they be so active *and* be cold-blooded?

The answer lies in the huge size of many dinosaurs. There are no creatures quite like them alive today. But there is evidence that being cold-blooded does not rule out that a creature can be active and energetic and maintain a constant body temperature. Instead of obtaining most of its body heat from its own internal metabolism, as with warm-blooded creatures, cold-blooded creatures may use a method called gigantothermy to maintain their temperature.

Gigantothermy relies on a combination of biologic and environmental factors to work:[10]

A warm, temperate, or subtropical climate, such as that enjoyed by the dinosaurs. Heat absorbed during the day would be retained for many hours past dark in a large dinosaur.[11]

Large body size. The larger the body, the more likely it would be to retain heat absorbed from the environment or produced internally through normal metabolic processes.

Layers of body insulation. Layers of fat and the mere volume of the gut of the armored and plated dinosaurs were probably responsible for retaining body heat. Armor plating may have added to their insulation.

A digestive process producing heat. Armored, plated, and bone-headed dinosaurs digested their food using a fermentation process that naturally produced heat as a by-product.

Special adaptations of the circulatory system. Blood flow and the circulatory path were used to pass heat from the core or gut of the dinosaur to its surface where it could be safely shed to avoid overheating. The extensive surface area of the body, including their long tails, plates, and armor, may have been part of this strategy for shedding excess heat.

All of the above reasons made it possible for large dinosaurs to maintain high body temperatures while still having lower cold-blooded metabolic rates. This could have made a significant difference in the survival of the armored and plated dinosaurs, because a lower metabolism required them to eat less than they would have needed if they had been warm-blooded. Lower food requirements would have allowed a larger population to be supported than if metabolic rates and food requirements were higher.

But the theory of gigantothermy comes with a significant problem. It does not account for the metabolic process of a small dinosaur or a large dinosaur while it was young and growing, before it reached a size at which gigantothermy could take over. This remains one of the puzzles of dinosaur metabolism. Perhaps the warm environment was enough to keep them active. This, plus the fact that they were eating more as they grew, might account for their maintaining a constant body temperature without the benefit of gigantothermy.

Speed

Dinosaur speed can be calculated if a scientist has trackways of a dinosaur and an accurate measurement of the length of its limbs. Trackways are a series of footprints made by a dinosaur in the mud, which became fossilized. Many trackways associated with ankylosaurs have been found around the world. Few, if any, have been found for the stegosaurs and pachycephalosaurs.

Trackways are not so important for understanding the speed of these creatures, however, because their anatomy can tell us much about how they moved. The four-legged armored and plated dinosaurs had heavy legs designed more for carrying their great weight than for speed. In fact, with front legs that sprawled somewhat to the sides, these animals were probably incapable of running very fast at all. They were most likely faster than sauropods but slower than ceratopsians and bipedal dinosaurs.

The pachycephalosaurs, although two-legged, were not built for speed, either. Their legs were built for strength, a characteristic that probably served them well when they engaged in head-butting contests. But the upper bones of the leg were longer than the lower, making it difficult for them to run very fast for long periods. They were certainly slower than any predators of their day.

Males and Females

Telling males from females is not easy from skeletons. Paleontologists can be comfortable about doing this only when an abundance of skeletons from the same kind of

Pachycephalosaurus

Gastonia   *Huayangosaurus*

The armored and plated dinosaurs had heavy legs designed more for carrying their heavy weight than for speed. They were not fast runners. Neither were the two-legged pachycephalosaurs, whose legs were built for strength rather than speed.

dinosaur can be compared. They look for differences that could distinguish the males from the females. These traits are the result of sexual dimorphism—naturally occurring differences between the sexes of the same kind of animal. These traits may be in size, shape, or behavioral differences. In nature, these differences help identify the males from the females and may also have other important functions. For example, male elephants have tusks that are used during combat or jousting with other males. Male deer have antlers to lock and wrestle with rivals to win the favor of a female.

In the fossils of some kinds of dinosaurs, there are obvious differences that suggest which ones are males and which are females. Paleontologist Peter Dodson did an extensive study of the horned dinosaur *Protoceratops* and showed that the size and showiness of the frill probably distinguished males from females. Adult specimens of *Protoceratops* can be divided into two groups based on the size of the frill. He felt that the dinosaurs with the larger frills were the males.[12] Crested duck-billed dinosaurs are another group in which abundant skeletal specimens provide clues to separating males from females.

Corythosaurus, Lambeosaurus, and *Parasaurolophus* are all examples of duck-billed dinosaurs whose skulls show two distinctly different crest shapes as a result of sexual dimorphism.

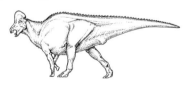

Corythosaurus

There are no obvious clues to sexual differences among specimens of armored and plated dinosaurs, even for those such as *Euoplocephalus* for which there are many skull specimens available. The bone-headed dinosaurs, on the other hand, have yielded some interesting clues to which were males and which were females.

There is probably more available fossil evidence for the pachycephalosaur *Stegoceras* than any other bone-headed dinosaur. More than two dozen skulls and skull fragments have been found for this dinosaur. Paleontologist Ralph Chapman conducted a study of the skulls and found that they could be divided into two groups: those with a thick-walled dome and those with a thinner dome. He concluded that the ones with the thicker domes were males due to the belief that they used their heads to butt rival males.[13]

CHAPTER 6

EGGS AND BABIES

Dinosaurs, like their bird descendants and most known reptiles, hatched from eggs. More than 230 dinosaur egg sites have been discovered, and three quarters of these are from North America and Asia.[1] Most that have been found date from the Late Cretaceous Period.

Fossil dinosaur eggs come in various shapes and sizes, including round, oval, and elongated oval varieties.[2] The smallest known dinosaur eggs are round and only about 3 inches (7.6 centimeters) in diameter. The largest, found in China, are elongate and about 18 inches (46 centimeters) long.

Dinosaurs laid their eggs in one of two basic patterns: clutches (groups) of eggs and eggs laid in rows. The fact that any dinosaur eggs became fossilized at all seems miraculous because of their delicate nature. Yet a number of natural forces have managed to preserve many such eggs in rock for us to examine today. Some were buried by sudden sandstorms and falling sand dunes, dooming many dinosaurs along with their unhatched young.[3] Other nesting sites in the world, such as

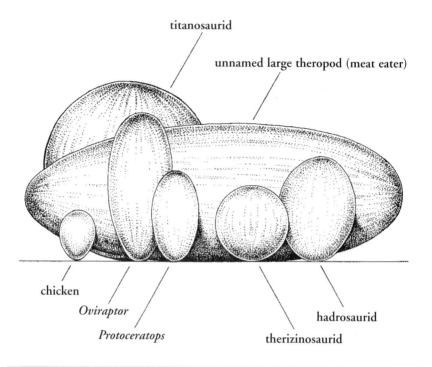

titanosaurid

unnamed large theropod (meat eater)

chicken

Oviraptor

Protoceratops

hadrosaurid

therizinosaurid

Shapes of various kinds of eggs including those of sauropod dinosaurs, a chicken, the horned dinosaur *Protoceratops*, *Oviraptor*, and a therizinosaur dinosaur (shown to scale).

those found in France, India, and northwestern North America, became fossilized not only because of sandstorms but also as a result of mud slides and other rapidly occurring natural catastrophes that quickly buried the eggs and nests.

There are no reports of fossil eggs for armored, plated, or bone-headed dinosaurs. Being ornithischians, it is possible that their eggs were similar to those of distantly related horned or ornithopod dinosaurs. Dinosaur egg expert Ken Carpenter suggests that their eggs would have been round. They would also have varied in size depending on the size of the dinosaur in question, ranging perhaps from about the size of an orange to a grapefruit.[4] But Carpenter and other scientists really do not think that they know enough to make an accurate guess about the eggs of these dinosaurs. Finding eggs of the armored and plated dinosaurs has been made even more challenging because many lived so much longer ago in the Jurassic Period than those dinosaurs for whom eggs are most frequently found. Discovering the eggs and nests of armored, plated, or bone-headed dinosaurs is a worthy challenge for any paleontologist.

Even though nesting sites for these dinosaurs have not yet been discovered, there are a few known specimens of baby or juvenile armored and plated dinosaurs. A young stegosaur from Utah has been pieced together from several specimens, including evidence of plates, and measures about 5 feet (1.5 meters) long.[5] A nodosaur "scuteling" from Texas measuring only about 20 inches (51 centimeters) long is known from limb and vertebrae pieces.[6] Neither of these young dinosaurs included evidence of dermal armor or plates.

It would be interesting to know how quickly the Ankylosauria developed their extensive armor plating. Were they born with armor or did it grow over time as the animal matured? A remarkable set of specimens of the Chinese ankylosaur *Pinacosaurus* provides some answers to these questions. More than fifteen specimens, ranging from juveniles to adults, have been found. Paleontologist Ken Carpenter has studied these dinosaurs to see how the armor plating and tail club developed as the animals grew. At about 5 feet (1.5 meters) long—a little less than half the size of an adult—*Pinacosaurus* showed the beginning growth of armor plating on its snout and neck, but no tail club was present. When the dinosaur grew a little more, to about 7.5 feet (2.3 meters) long, armor was present on most of the skull bones, some body armor was present, and the tail club was beginning to grow. When *Pinacosaurus* reached nearly adult size, at about 10 feet (3 meters) long, the skull and body were completely armored and the tail club had reached its full size.[7]

CHAPTER 7

FEEDING HABITS AND ADAPTATIONS

The plant-eating armored, plated, and bone-headed dinosaurs were equipped with simple but effective jaws and teeth. The teeth of these creatures varied in size and number for each of these kinds of dinosaurs, but they shared some common characteristics. The teeth were packed along the side of the jaw area, suggesting that these creatures had fleshy cheeks for holding food that was being chewed. The teeth were set in rows and were shaped something like a spatula with a ridge over the triangular top edge to aid in tearing vegetation. These were not grinding teeth like those of the duckbills and iguanodonts. Grinding was probably done in the stomach with the aid of stones, or gastroliths, that were rolled around by the muscular action of the stomach, crushing food between the rock surfaces. Evidence for gastroliths has been found with specimens of *Stegosaurus* and the ankylosaur *Panoplosaurus*. In addition to the action of stomach stones, the stegosaurs and especially the ankylosaurs had huge guts in which the natural digestive fermentation of food would have taken place slowly but effectively.[1]

The Ankylosauria and Stegosauria were aided by having toothless beaks to snip and trim twigs and branches from low-lying vegetation. These animals are known as low browsers, meaning that most of what they ate grew close to the ground. This has been deduced because of their body structure, with short front legs and a low-slung head. The normal foraging height for these creatures would have been about three feet (one meter) off the ground.[2] You can readily see that the taller duckbills and iguanodonts occupied a foraging niche a little higher than the armored and plated dinosaurs, and the sauropods had an even loftier reach.

It has been suggested that *Stegosaurus* could rear up on its hind legs to reach higher plants, and it seems likely that it could have done so since its center of gravity was situated near its hind legs.[3] Ankylosaurs were somewhat bulkier than stegosaurs, and it may have been more difficult for them to shift their weight back in order to rear up. Most scientists are comfortable viewing these creatures as low browsers. The anatomy of the ankylosaur skull, with its extensive nasal passages, shows that these creatures could have easily eaten and breathed at the same time. The beak was broader and more scooplike than the stegosaurs', and ankylosaurs probably had a long, flexible tongue to help them handle incoming food.[4]

The pachycephalosaurs had similar eating habits to the armored and plated dinosaurs. They were not very tall, so they

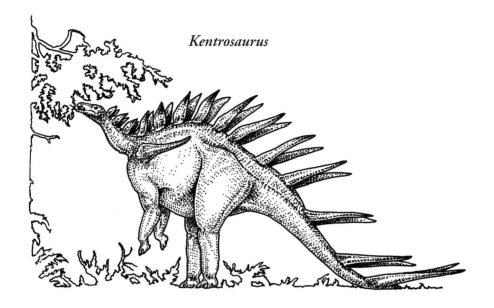

Kentrosaurus

Euoplocephalus

Kentrosaurus, a stegosaur, could probably rear up on its hind legs to reach higher plants. This would have been more difficult for the bulkier and lower ankylosaurs. The scoop-like beak of the ankylosaurs, such as *Euoplocephalus*, may have had a long, flexible tongue to help grab plants.

probably browsed on plants three feet (a meter) or so above the ground. Their teeth were divided into two basic groups. Small front teeth were sharp and could grasp and tear plants. The rear teeth were positioned in the cheeks and had triangular ridges for shredding vegetation. These animals were able to pluck and puncture leaves and small fruits with their front teeth and shred them with their cheek teeth. Their wide rib cage suggests that the bone-headed dinosaurs had a large gut for fermenting swallowed food.[5]

What Did They Eat?

The armored, plated, and bone-headed dinosaurs were all low-browsing animals, picking plants from ground cover, bushes, and other material at the base of the herbivory. They ate below the line of plants normally consumed by the taller sauropods, hadrosaurs, and iguanodonts. They probably plowed into the vegetation with their sharp beaks, snipping off branches and twigs with a snap of the jaws and a sideways pull of the head.

Although they lacked the more efficient plant grinding machinery of their ornithischian cousins, the armored, plated, and bone-headed dinosaurs were obviously successful and survived in one form or another for many millions of years.

Plant life on Earth changed dramatically during the rise and evolution of these dinosaurs. Three major kinds of land plants were common during the Jurassic and Cretaceous Periods during which they lived. Their diet may have consisted in part of the following menu:[6]

Pteridophytes. Pteridophytes included the ferns,

horsetails, and club mosses. Ferns came in forms that hugged the ground but also as trees with an unadorned stemlike trunk with a single growing point at the top. These plants generally required a moist environment, but they were fast-growing and could be grazed without killing the plant, making them an excellent renewable source of food. These plants were abundant throughout the age of dinosaurs. These were an especially important source of food for lower-browsing armored, plated, and bone-headed dinosaurs.

Gymnosperms. Gymnosperms were two groups of primitive seed plants, the conifers and the cycads. They reproduced by means of a naked seed, in contrast to the angiosperms, which had a seed enclosed within a fruit. Today's conifers, including pine trees and other evergreens, existed in the form of small shrubs and large trees. Another branch of the conifer group included the cypress and bald cypress families and broad-leaved ginkgo trees. The cycads were mostly short plants with bulbous or palmlike trunks. They were capped with fronds reminiscent of palm trees.

Gymnosperms were not moist or soft. They were not an easy food to digest, nor did they contain abundant nutrients. They were gradually displaced as a source of food by the rise of the flowering plants, or angiosperms, in the late part of the Cretaceous Period.

Angiosperms. Angiosperms were flowering plants, the last of the major plant groups to evolve. They were distinguished by having a seed borne within a fruit, unlike the gymnosperms, which bore naked seeds. They first appeared in

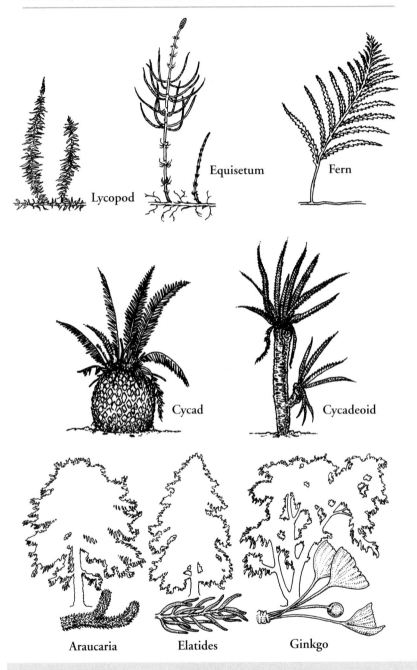

Lycopod

Equisetum

Fern

Cycad

Cycadeoid

Araucaria

Elatides

Ginkgo

Some land plants that were common during the time of the armored, plated, and bone-headed dinosaurs.

the middle of the Cretaceous Period. They diversified and spread rapidly in the form of flowering shrubs to become the dominant plant group by the end of the Cretaceous Period.[7] They reproduced and grew more quickly than gymnosperms, making them abundantly available as dinosaur food. The foliage of angiosperms was generally more digestible, moist, and nutritionally sound than either pteridophytes or gymnosperms. The ability of these plants to spread and grow quickly made them ideally suited for the veggie-munching machinery of the plant-eating dinosaurs.

CHAPTER 8

ARMOR, CLUBS, SPIKES, AND PLATES—THE DECORATIONS OF DEFENSE

Imagine a large, hungry meat eater in search of its next meal. If it lived in western North America during the Late Jurassic Period, it might have been *Allosaurus*. In its search for food it runs across an adult *Stegosaurus* quietly eating from the fronds of some low-lying ferns. As it approaches from behind, hoping to pounce on this peaceful plant eater, the stegosaur picks up its scent and becomes aware of the meat eater's presence. *Allosaurus* suddenly notices its prey's posture change. The

Stegosaurus turns its head to view the *Allosaurus* over its shoulder. It stands taller on its stiff legs, perhaps even taking in a deep breath to inflate its abdomen and give the appearance of being even larger than it is. Its back plates stand erect and flex slowly from side to side. Then it begins to sharply flex its tail back and forth, warding off the meat eater with four long, sharp tail spikes that swing back and forth at about the height of the predator's knees. To get to the vulnerable part of the *Stegosaurus*, the allosaur would have to avoid those spikes and fight through the flapping back plates to make an effective

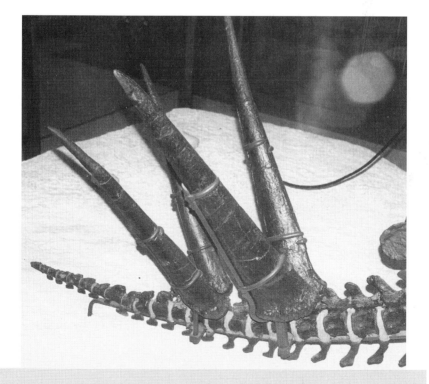

Stegosaurus could ward off a predator by swinging its four sharp tail spikes.

strike with its claws and teeth. One clean hit from the stegosaur's spikes and *Allosaurus* would suffer a painful wound that might take a long while to heal, perhaps even threatening its life.

The *Stegosaurus* is way too much trouble today. *Allosaurus* is not that desperate for food. It walks on to find something to eat that is less threatening, perhaps a young sauropod that has wandered away from its herd.

Although *Stegosaurus* did not have extensive body armor other than patches of small bony knobs, its plates and spikes were probably adequate in most defensive situations. The back plates of *Stegosaurus* were particularly large. Those of most

The back plates of *Stegosaurus* could make the animal look larger and more dangerous when viewed from the side. The dinosaur may have also been able to change the color of its plates if it was excited or felt threatened.

other stegosaurs were smaller and more pointed but provided the same visual effect as those on *Stegosaurus*. They made the animal appear larger when viewed from the side.

Armored and plated dinosaur expert Ken Carpenter believes that intimidation was probably an important part of the defense of these creatures. He thinks that the plates could have been even more threatening if they could have changed color when the animal was angry or getting ready to defend itself. This idea is not so far-fetched when you remember that the plates were interwoven with a matrix of blood vessels. A sudden rush of blood to the plates could make them "blush" or change color, a clear warning to stay away.[1]

Now, imagine it is 70 million years later in the Late Cretaceous Period in North America, and imagine *Albertosaurus*, a large tyrannosaur from Canada, is searching for food. It comes across a solitary nodosaur, *Edmontonia*. This armored dinosaur also has a great sense of smell and immediately drops down to the ground in a defensive posture when the predator approaches. Its entire upper body is covered with armor. Its head is shielded by thick bony plates that cannot be bitten through. Its neck and shoulders are covered with large plates and spikes to prevent injury to the tender parts below. *Albertosaurus* can step on it but the nodosaur is so large and reinforced by its armor that the weight of the predator would have little effect. Furthermore, *Edmontonia* likes to rise up quickly on its muscular front legs and swing its shoulder spikes menacingly in the face of a tyrannosaur. This is one touchy fellow.

Ankylosaurus tail club

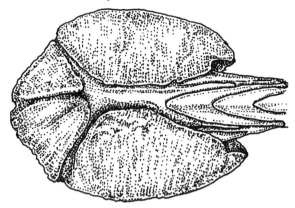

Euoplocephalus tail club

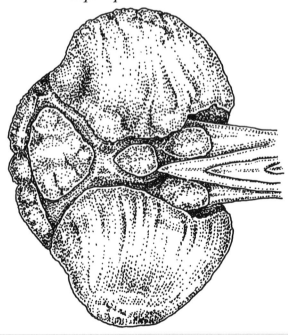

The heavy tail club of an ankylosaur was an effective weapon against a meat-eating attacker. Shown here are tail clubs of *Ankylosaurus* (top) and *Euoplocephalus*.

Losing patience with an uncooperative *Edmontonia*, *Albertosaurus* spies the ankylosaur *Euoplocephalus* walking across an open field and decides to try its luck with it. Like *Edmontonia*, its upper body is shielded by armor, but it lacks the large spikes around its head. Perhaps there is a chance that *Albertosaurus* can penetrate the neck armor with its teeth. However, *Euoplocephalus* has a large tail club that it now waves threateningly. As *Albertosaurus* leans down to snap at the rear of the animal, the club glances off its jaw, jarring loose a couple of teeth. If the predator walks any closer to attack its head, the tail club will be able to strike the leg. That could possibly break the leg, crippling *Albertosaurus* and sealing its doom.

The tyrannosaur decides to take its sore mouth and look elsewhere for food.

The heavily armored Ankylosauria must have been the most frustrating of all prey. What the nodosaurs lacked in a tail club they gained in the presence of more and larger spikes and horny knobs. The spines on some nodosaurs aimed upward, while in others they stuck out from the sides or formed a ring around the neck. The neck spines of *Edmontonia* could have been thrust at a predator to ward it off.[2]

If stegosaurs had been able to "blush" by changing the color of their back plates, what of the Ankylosauria? Ken Carpenter believes the same might have been true for the armor of the ankylosaurs and nodosaurs. It, too, was heavily vascularized, making it possible that the plates could change color due to a rapid infusion of blood from an excited heart.

In addition to tail clubs and back armor, nodosaurs often had large protruding spikes. The spikes on some nodosaurs aimed upward while in others they stuck out from the sides or formed a ring around the neck.

A predatory dinosaur in the Late Cretaceous Period of North America may have had better luck attacking the bone-headed dinosaurs. While their thick skullcaps were suited for head-butting contests with those of their own kind, head butting would not have been an effective defense against a charging meat eater about ten times its size. Bone-headed or not, the otherwise defenseless pachycephalosaur would probably have made a tender meal when compared to the stegosaurs and ankylosaurs.

CHAPTER 9

EXTINCTION OF THE DINOSAURS

Except for the survival of birds, the last of the dinosaurs became extinct 65 million years ago. However, dinosaurs did not disappear because they were evolutionary failures. Dinosaurs were one of the most successful forms of life ever to inhabit our planet. They ruled the earth for 160 million years. By comparison, humans and even our most distant relatives have been around for only about 4 million years.

Extinction is the irreversible elimination of an entire species of plant or animal. Once it occurs, there is no turning back. It is also a natural process. More than 99 percent of all the species of organisms that have ever lived on our planet are now extinct.[1]

Although the dinosaurs existed for so many millions of years, most species existed for only a few million years at a time, until they became extinct or evolved into improved versions that adapted to changes in the environment. So, to say that all the dinosaurs became extinct at the end of the Cretaceous Period is incorrect—most kinds of dinosaurs had already come and gone by then. There is no denying, though, that a mass extinction occurred at the end of the Cretaceous that wiped out about 65 to 70 percent of all animal life.[2] Even those groups of animals that survived—including frogs, lizards, turtles, salamanders, birds, insects, fish, crocodiles, alligators, and mammals—lost great numbers of their species.

Chief among the causes of animal extinction are environmental changes that affect their food supply or body chemistry (such as sustained changes in climate), disease, and natural disasters (such as volcanic eruptions, earthquakes, and the changing surface of Earth). Extensive hunting by natural enemies may also contribute to extinction. Humankind, for example, has hunted many animals such as the buffalo to extinction or near extinction.

Why did the last of the dinosaurs become extinct? This is a great mystery of science.

The death of the dinosaurs is difficult to explain because dinosaurs were part of a strangely selective extinction event. Any suitable explanation must account for the disappearance of dinosaurs as well as flying reptiles, reptiles that swam in the oceans, ammonites, and other sea creatures including some types of clams, mollusks, and plankton. One must also explain why so many other types of animals continued to thrive after the extinction of the dinosaurs.

Theories of Dinosaur Extinction

THEORY	TYPE OF THEORY	PROBLEMS WITH THE THEORY
The Big Rumble Smoke and dust spewed by mass volcanic eruptions shrouded the earth in darkness, killing plants, poisoning the air and water, and causing the climate to cool.	Gradual	Does not explain why other land- and ocean-dwelling animals survived.
Shifting Continents Planetary cooling caused by shifting continents and changes to the earth's oceans. Water between the land masses would have cooled the air and caused wind.	Gradual	This happened very slowly. Why couldn't dinosaurs and marine reptiles have adapted to the climate change or moved to warmer climates?
Pesky Mammals New mammals stole and ate dinosaur eggs.	Gradual	Does not explain why some sea life became extinct or why other egg-laying land animals such as snakes and lizards survived. Also, small mammals coexisted with dinosaurs for many millions of year without this happening.
Flower Poisoning Flowers first appeared during the Cretaceous Period. Were dinosaurs unable to adapt to the chemical makeup of this new source of food?	Gradual	Plant-eating dinosaurs actually increased in diversity and numbers during the rise of the flowering plants.
Bombardment from Space Impact by an asteroid or comet shrouded the earth in darkness from debris thrown into the atmosphere and may have poisoned the air. Plants died and the climate cooled.	Sudden	Although theory is favored by scientists, it does not explain survival of some land reptiles, mammals, birds, amphibians, and plants, or why certain ocean life perished but not others.
Supernova Explosion of a nearby star bathed the earth in deadly cosmic rays.	Sudden	Why did some life-forms die and not others?

Theories

Paleontologists disagree on the causes of dinosaur extinction and the length of time it took for this mass dying to occur. There are many theories about what happened. They come in two basic varieties: gradual causes and sudden causes.

Gradual causes would have required millions of years of change. Some possible gradual causes include global climate changes (warming or cooling), volcanic action, shifting continents, overpopulation, poisoning by flowering plants, and the appearance of egg-stealing mammals.

Sudden or catastrophic causes would have taken no longer than a few years to wipe out the dinosaurs. One of the most popular extinction theories concerns the collision of an asteroid or comet with Earth.

So far, no single extinction theory can fully explain the great dying at the end of the age of dinosaurs. Evidence has been mounting in favor of the asteroid theory. But a collision with an asteroid may have only been the final blow in a gradual extinction that had been mounting for many years. The asteroid theory also fails to explain why the extinction was so selective. Why did marine reptiles die but most fish survive? Why did dinosaurs of all sizes disappear but birds continue to thrive? There are still many questions to answer before scientists totally understand this great mystery.

CHAPTER 10

MAJOR DISCOVERIES

This chapter summarizes the major discoveries of the armored, plated, and bone-headed dinosaurs. It chronicles the most important and complete specimens of armored, plated, and bone-headed dinosaurs that have been discovered, when and where they were found, and the people who identified them.

✦ ✦ ✦

1833 (England)—*Hylaeosaurus* ("wood lizard") was among the first three dinosaurs ever named and was the first known armored dinosaur. Our knowledge of this early nodosaur is based on two fragmentary skeletons that included evidence of armor plates. It was named by **Gideon Mantell**, the British physician who also named *Iguanodon* ("iguana tooth").

✦ ✦ ✦

1867 (England)—British scientist **Thomas Huxley** named *Acanthopholis* ("spiny scales") after the large armor plates that were found with this fragmentary skeleton of a nodosaur.

1874 (England)—*Craterosaurus* ("skull lizard") is notable for being the first stegosaur named, although so little of it was discovered that its true nature has never been fully known. It was named by British paleontologist **Harry G. Seeley.**

1877 (United States)—*Stegosaurus* ("roofed lizard") was one of the most remarkable dinosaurs named by **Othniel C. Marsh.** The species is represented by two nearly complete and several partial skeletons. Equipped with its large back plates and spikes on its tail, *Stegosaurus* was the first good example of an armored or plated dinosaur. It lived during the Late Jurassic Period.

1889 (United States)—*Nodosaurus* ("knobby lizard") was discovered in Wyoming and named by **Othniel C. Marsh.** Though incomplete, it was the best example of a nodosaur at the time. The name Nodosauridae was used by Marsh to categorize the first known members of the armored dinosaur group.

1902 (England)—The stegosaur *Dacentrurus* ("very spiked tail") was similar to *Stegosaurus*, but instead of plates running along its back, it had large spikes. It was named by **Frederick A. Lucas** and was the most complete dinosaur of its kind found in England by that time. It dates from the Late Jurassic

Period, making it one of the oldest known members of the stegosaur family.

✦ ✦ ✦

1902 **(Canada)**—The 6-foot- (1.8-meter-) long *Stegoceras* ("covered horn") was the first bone-headed dinosaur found, although its partial remains fooled its discoverer, **Lawrence Lambe**, into thinking that he had discovered a horned dinosaur. Later discoveries showed that the bony crown Lambe had originally thought was the base of a horn was actually a dome on the top of its head. An abundance of fossil evidence now makes *Stegoceras* one of the best understood pachycephalosaurs.

✦ ✦ ✦

1908 **(United States)**—*Ankylosaurus* ("armored lizard") was discovered and named by **Barnum Brown**. Even though it is

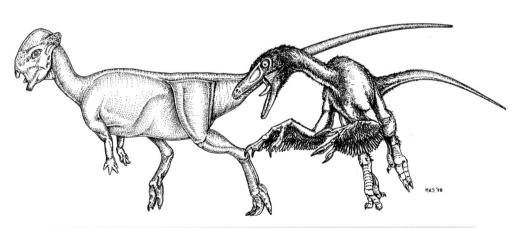

Stegoceras is chased by *Saurornitholestes.*

the most famous armored dinosaur, it is known from only three incomplete skeletons, including partial skulls. At about 25 feet (7.5 meters) long, it was one of the largest ankylosaurs. It was distinguished from nodosaurs by the bony club on its tail.

1910 **(Canada)**—*Euoplocephalus* ("well-armed head") is one of best known ankylosaurs. More than forty specimens have been found, including fifteen complete or partial skulls. One specimen was found with its body armor in place. This Late Cretaceous armored dinosaur was named by **Lawrence Lambe**

Euoplocephalus could possibly knock *Albertosaurus* off its feet with a swing of its tail club.

and discovered in Alberta. This dinosaur almost went by the name of *Stereocephalus*, but Lambe found out that this name had already been given to an insect.[1]

1915 (Tanzania)—*Kentrosaurus* ("spiked lizard") is from the stegosaur family. It is known from two adult specimens composed of pieces of several individuals and many isolated remains. It had two rows of plates running down its neck, followed by two rows of long spikes extending the length of its tail. It was discovered in East Africa and named by German fossil hunter **Edwin Hennig**.

1919 (Canada)—**Lawrence Lambe** named *Panoplosaurus* ("fully armored lizard"), a nodosaur from western Canada. This medium- to large-sized armored dinosaur from the Late Cretaceous Period was up to 23 feet (7 meters) long and had bony plates on its back and fused to its skull.

1928 (Canada)—*Edmontonia* ("from the Horseshoe Canyon formation of the Edmonton formation") was an armored dinosaur of the nodosaur group. It was named by **Charles M. Sternberg** after the Edmonton Formation in Alberta, Canada, where it was found. One remarkable specimen includes fossilized back and head armor. It dates from the Late Cretaceous Period.

1933 (China)—*Pinacosaurus* ("board lizard"), a medium-sized ankylosaur about 18 feet (5.4 meters) long, was named by **Charles W. Gilmore**. It is known from more than fifteen specimens. It had a bony tail club. It was the first armored dinosaur discovered in Central Asia and dates from the Late Cretaceous Period.

1943 (United States)—*Pachycephalosaurus* ("thick-headed lizard"), the dinosaur after which the group of bone-headed dinosaurs was named, was discovered in the western United States and named by **Barnum Brown** and **Erich M. Schlaikjer**. The specimen is only represented by a complete skull and the remains of several bony skullcaps. Judging from the size of the skull relative to other better known bone-headed dinosaurs, *Pachycephalosaurus* was the largest dinosaur of this type at about 15 feet (4.5 meters) long.

1952 (China)—The ankylosaur *Talarurus* ("basket tail") was named by Russian paleontologist **Evgenii A. Maleev**. The name "basket tail" refers to the wickerlike appearance of the interlocking vertebrae and ossified tendons in the tail of ankylosaurs. This dinosaur is known from two partial skulls and a nearly complete skeleton and armor. The mounted skeleton of this dinosaur is a composite of five individuals found in the same bone bed.[2]

1970 **(United States)**—The nodosaur *Sauropelta* ("lizard shield") was named by American paleontologist **John Ostrom**. It was a medium-sized armored dinosaur about 19 feet (5.8 meters) long and is known from several partial skeletons, two crushed skulls, and remains of armor plating. It lived during the Early Cretaceous Period.

1973 **(China)**—The Chinese stegosaur *Wuerhosaurus* ("Wuerho lizard") was named by Chinese paleontologist **Dong Zhiming**. The partial specimen revealed a large plated dinosaur similar to *Stegosaurus*, but with smaller back plates. *Wuerhosaurus* is currently noteworthy because it is the latest known survivor of the stegosaur family. It lived during the Early Cretaceous Period, whereas most other known stegosaurs lived during the Middle and Late Jurassic Periods.

1974 **(China)**—Eight Polish-Mongolian paleontological expeditions led between 1961 and 1971 resulted in the discovery of three new pachycephalosaurs and two new armored dinosaurs (see **1977, China**). Dating from the Late Cretaceous Period, the pachycephalosaurs *Homalocephale* ("level head"), *Prenocephale* ("sloping head"), and *Tylocephale* ("swollen head") were all named by Polish paleontologists **Teresa Maryanska** and **Halzka Osmólska**. The best of those specimens was *Homalocephale*, consisting of a complete skull and nearly complete skeleton. It was a small bipedal dinosaur measuring about 10 feet (3 meters) long and was a member of a branch of bone-headed dinosaurs whose domes were not as large or thick as their pachycephalosaurian relatives. The scientists named these dinosaurs after the level, sloping, and swollen shapes of their bony domed skulls.

1977 (China)—The ankylosaurs *Tarchia* ("brainy one") and *Saichania* ("beautiful one") were also discovered during the Polish-Mongolian paleontological expeditions to Mongolia and were named by **Teresa Maryanska** in 1977. Both date from the Late Cretaceous Period. *Tarchia* is known from seven specimens that include complete and partial skulls, skeletons, and armor. *Tarchia* is the largest known armored dinosaur from Asia and measured about 28 feet (8.5 meters) long. *Saichania* is also known from several specimens that include armor and two complete skulls. It was about 23 feet (7 meters) long and had many knobs and spikes along its body to protect its head, back, and stomach. Both *Tarchia* and *Saichania* had bulbous armor knobs on the front and top of their skulls and bony tail clubs.

1977 (China)—The stegosaur *Tuojiangosaurus* ("Tuo River lizard") is understood from two partial skeletons and is currently the best known stegosaur from China. It dates from the Late Jurassic Period. It had two rows of small triangular plates running down its back and four spikes on its tail. It was about 23 feet (7 meters) long and was named by Chinese paleontologists **Dong Zhiming, Li X, Zhou Shiwu,** and **Zhang Yihong.**

1977 (China)—*Wannanosaurus* ("Wannan lizard") was the smallest and most primitive member of the pachycephalosaurians. It was only about 2 feet (0.6 meters) long and had a much less developed dome on top of its head than its pachycephalosaur relatives. It was discovered by **Hou Lianhai**.

✦   ✦   ✦

1978 (China)—*Micropachycephalosaurus* ("tiny thick-headed lizard") is one of the tiniest known dinosaurs but has the longest name of any dinosaur. The bipedal creature measured only about 20 inches (51 centimeters) long and was a pachycephalosaur. Its fragmentary remains are not good enough to determine if it was a member of the more primitive flat-headed pachycephalosaurs or the domed variety. The specimen is now thought to be that of a juvenile.[3] It was named by **Dong Zhiming**.

✦   ✦   ✦

1980 (Australia)—*Minmi* (after Minmi Crossing in Australia), a small nodosaur measuring about 7 feet (2.1 meters) long, was found in Queensland, Australia. It was the first undeniable armored dinosaur discovered in the Southern Hemisphere. Its name, which happens to be the shortest for any dinosaur, was given to it by paleontologist **Ralph Molnar**. *Minmi* lived during the Early Cretaceous Period. Three specimens of this dinosaur are currently known.

1982 (China)—*Huayangosaurus* ("Huayang lizard") is the only member of a family of the most primitive stegosaurs. Dating from the Middle Jurassic Period in China, it was about 13 feet (4 meters) long. It had a paired row of pointed spines on its back, four tail spikes, and one large spike protruding from each of its shoulders. It was named by **Dong Zhiming, Tang Zhilu,** and **Zhou Shiwu.**

✦ ✦ ✦

1982 (China)—*Goyocephale* ("decorated head") is another member of the family of primitive flat-headed pachycephalosaurians. This small bone-headed dinosaur measured about 10 feet (3 meters) long and was named by the Mongolian paleontologist **Altangerel Perle** and Polish paleontologists **Teresa Maryanska** and **Halzka Osmólska.**

✦ ✦ ✦

1983 (China)—*Shamosaurus* ("desert lizard") was a heavy-bodied ankylosaur from Asia. Its name refers to the Gobi Desert region of Mongolia where the specimen was found. It had neck armor and bony horns pointing rearward from its back. Russian **Tatiana Tumanova** named this dinosaur.

✦ ✦ ✦

1993 (China)—*Tianchiasaurus* ("heavenly pool lizard") was named by **Dong Zhiming** for a famous lake in China near the location of the fossils. This 10-foot- (3-meter-) long ankylosaur was one of the first armored dinosaurs and lived during the Middle Jurassic Period.

1993 **(China)**—*Tsagantegia* (for Tsagan Teg) was named by Russian paleontologist **Tatiana Tumanova** after the Tsagan Teg mountain region near the location of the fossils. This was a very large ankylosaur with a long snout and prominent armor around its eyes.

1994 **(United States)**—*Mymoorapelta* ("shield of Mygatt-Moore"), was named by **James Kirkland** and **Kenneth Carpenter** after the families (the Mygatts and the Moores) who discovered the fossil locality. It is the earliest known ankylosaur found in North America and dates from the Late Jurassic Period of Colorado. It had triangular neck spines, tail spines, and fused armor on its back, but it is more primitive than other North American ankylosaurs.

1995 **(United States)**—The nodosaur *Texasetes* ("Texas dweller") was named by **Walter P. Coombs, Jr.** This specimen is based on fragmentary evidence. The dinosaur lived in the Early Cretaceous Period.

1996 **(United States)**—The nodosaur *Pawpawsaurus* ("formation lizard") was found in Texas and named by **Yuong Nam Lee.** Its remarkably preserved skull provided the first evidence of bony eyelid armor in nodosaurs.

1998 (China)—*Shanxia* ("of Shanxi province") was a Chinese ankylosaur from the Late Cretaceous with horns projecting outward from the back of its head. It was a small armored dinosaur, about 12 feet (3.6 meters) long. It was named by **Paul Barrett, You Hailu, Paul Upchurch,** and **Alex Burton.**

✦ ✦ ✦

1998 (China)—*Tianzhenosaurus* ("Tianzhen lizard") named by **Pang Qiqing** and **Cheng Zhengwu** after Tianzhen county in Sichuan Province, China. It was an ankylosaur similar to *Shanxia* and found at a different locality in the same fossil formation. Some scientists think it is the same dinosaur as *Shanxia*. The specimen is about 10 feet (3 meters) long and includes a nearly complete skull and skeleton.

✦ ✦ ✦

1998 (United States)—The ankylosaur *Gargoyleosaurus* ("gargoyle lizard") was described by **Kenneth Carpenter, Clifford Miles,** and **Karen Cloward.** Found in deposits from the Late Jurassic Period in Wyoming, this dinosaur has anatomical features that are like those of both nodosaurs and ankylosaurs. This specimen provides evidence that nodosaurs and ankylosaurs had a common ancestor. Its body armor included a covering of conelike knobs and long spines projecting from its shoulders.

1999 (United States)—*Nodocephalosaurus* ("knob-headed lizard") was named by **Robert M. Sullivan** and found in Late Cretaceous deposits in New Mexico. It is an ankylosaur based on an incomplete skull but shows some special features including large, bulging armor knobs on its skull roof and snout. It might be related to the Asian ankylosaurs *Saichania* and *Tarchia*, which also have unusual skull armor.

CURRENTLY KNOWN ARMORED, PLATED, AND BONE-HEADED DINOSAURS

The list below includes the genus names of currently known and scientifically accepted armored, plated, and bone-headed dinosaurs. Each genus name is followed by the name(s) of the paleontologist(s) who described it in print and the year in which it was named.

Ankylosauria

Acanthopholis—Huxley, 1867

Amtosaurus—Kurzanov and Tumanova, 1978

Ankylosaurus—Brown, 1908

Edmontonia—Sternberg, 1928

Euoplocephalus—Lambe, 1910

Gargoyleosaurus—Carpenter, Miles, and Cloward, 1998

Hoplitosaurus—Lucas, 1902

Hylaeosaurus—Mantell, 1833

Minmi—Molnar, 1980

Mymoorapelta—Kirkland and Carpenter, 1994

Nodosaurus—Marsh, 1889

Nodocephalosaurus—Sullivan, 1999

Panoplosaurus—Lambe, 1919

Pawpawsaurus—Lee, 1996

Pinacosaurus—Gilmore, 1933

Saichania—Maryanska, 1977

Sauropelta—Ostrom, 1970

Shamosaurus—Tumanova, 1983

Shanxia—Barrett, You, Upchurch, and Burton, 1998

Silvisaurus—Eaton, 1960

Talarurus—Maleev, 1952

Tarchia—Maryanska, 1977

Texasetes—Coombs, 1995

Tianchiasaurus—Dong, 1993

Tianzhenosaurus—Pang and Cheng, 1998

Tsagantegia—Tumanova, 1993

Stegosauria

Chialingosaurus—Young, 1959

Chungkingosaurus—Dong, Zhou, and Zhang, 1983

Craterosaurus—Seeley, 1874

Dacentrurus—Lucas, 1902

Dravidosaurus—Yadagiri and Ayyasami, 1979

Huayangosaurus—Dong, Tang, and Zhou, 1982

Kentrosaurus—Hennig, 1915

Lexovisaurus—Hoffstetter, 1957

Paranthodon—Nopcsa, 1929

Stegosaurus—Marsh, 1877

Tuojiangosaurus—Dong, Li, Zhou, and Zhang, 1977

Wuerhosaurus—Dong, 1973

Pachycephalosauria

Goyocephale—Perle, Maryanska, and Osmólska, 1982

Gravitholus—Wall and Galton, 1979

Homalocephale—Maryanska and Osmólska, 1974

Micropachycephalosaurus—Dong, 1978

Ornatotholus—Galton and Sues, 1983

Pachycephalosaurus—Brown and Schlaikjer, 1943

Prenocephale—Maryanska and Osmólska, 1974

Stegoceras—Lambe, 1902

Stygimoloch—Galton and Sues, 1983

Tylocephale—Maryanska and Osmólska, 1974

Wannanosaurus—Hou, 1977

Yaverlandia—Galton, 1971

Chapter Notes

Chapter 1. Dinosaurs Defined

1. Peter Dodson and Susan D. Dawson, "Making the Fossil Record of Dinosaurs," *Modern Geology*, 1991, vol. 16, p. 13.

Chapter 2. Origins and Evolution

1. David B. Weishampel, Peter Dodson, and Halszka Osmólska, eds., *The Dinosauria* (Berkeley, Calif.: University of California Press, 1990), p. 11.

2. Paul Sereno, "The Evolution of Dinosaurs," *Science*, June 25, 1999, vol. 284, p. 2137.

3. Ibid.

4. Weishampel, Dodson, and Osmólska, p. 433.

5. Based on Weishampel, Dodson, and Osmólska.

Chapter 4. Anatomy

1. Stephen Jay Gould, ed., *The Book of Life* (New York: W. W. Norton & Company, 1993), pp. 67–68.

2. James O. Farlow and Michael K. Brett-Surman, eds., *The Complete Dinosaur* (Bloomington: Indiana University Press, 1997), pp. 299–300.

3. Philip J. Currie and Kevin Padian, eds., *The Encyclopedia of Dinosaurs* (San Diego, Calif.: Academic Press, 1997), p. 16.

4. David B. Weishampel, Peter Dodson, and Halszka Osmólska, eds., *The Dinosauria* (Berkeley, Calif.: University of California Press, 1990), p. 482.

5. Ken Carpenter, "Agonistic Behavior In Pachycephalosaurs (Ornithischia: Dinosauria): A New Look At Head-Butting Behavior," *University of Wyoming, Contributions to Geology*, 1997, vol. 32, pp. 19–25.

6. Personal communication with Peter Dodson, November 27, 2000.

7. Currie and Padian, p. 703.

8. Ibid., p. 19.

9. Farlow and Brett-Surman, p. 311.

Chapter 5. Physiology

1. Philip J. Currie and Kevin Padian, eds., *The Encyclopedia of Dinosaurs* (San Diego, Calif.: Academic Press, 1997), p. 371.

2. David E. Fastovsky and David B. Weishampel, *The Evolution and Extinction of the Dinosaurs* (New York: Cambridge University Press, 1996), p. 339.

3. Charles Schuchert and Clara Mae Levene, *O.C. Marsh, Pioneer in Paleontology* (New Haven, Conn.: Yale University Press, 1940), pp. 405–406.

4. Fastovsky and Weishampel, p. 129.

5. Robert T. Bakker, *The Dinosaur Heresies* (New York: William Morrow and Company, 1986), p. 348.

6. John R. Horner and James Gorman, *Digging Dinosaurs* (New York: Workman, 1988), pp. 84–85.

7. Dale A. Russell, *An Odyssey in Time* (Toronto: University of Toronto Press, 1989), p. 150.

8. Fastovsky and Weishampel, based on Fig. 14.11, p. 346.

9. Mark A. Norell, Eugene S. Gaffney, and Lowell Dingus, *Discovering Dinosaurs in the American Museum of Natural History* (New York: Alfred A. Knopf, 1995), pp. 56–57.

10. James O. Farlow and Michael K. Brett-Surman, eds., *The Complete Dinosaur* (Bloomington: Indiana University Press, 1997), pp. 499–501.

11. Edwin H. Colbert, R. B. Cowles, and C. M. Bogert, "Temperature Tolerances in the American Alligator and their Bearing on the Habits, Evolution, and Extinction of the Dinosaurs," *American Museum of Natural History Bulletin 86*, 1946, pp. 327–374.

12. Peter Dodson, "Quantitative Aspects of Relative Growth and Sexual Dimorphism in *Protoceratops*," *Journal of Paleontology*, 1976, vol. 50, pp. 929–940.

13. Fastovsky and Weishampel, pp. 163–164.

Chapter 6. Eggs and Babies

1. Kenneth Carpenter, *Eggs, Nests, and Baby Dinosaurs* (Bloomington: Indiana University Press, 1999), pp. 8–30.

2. Kenneth Carpenter, Karl F. Hirsch, and John R. Horner, *Dinosaur Eggs and Babies* (New York: Cambridge University Press, 1994), p. 1.

3. Zhiming Dong and Philip J. Currie, "On the Discovery of an Oviraptorid Skeleton on a Nest of Eggs at Bayan Mandahu, Inner Mongolia, People's Republic of China," *Canadian Journal of Earth Sciences*, 1996, no. 70, p. 508.

4. Personal communication with Kenneth Carpenter, August 24, 2000.

5. Ibid.

6. Carpenter, Hirsch, and Horner, pp. 18–21.

7. Personal communication with Kenneth Carpenter, August 11, 2000.

Chapter 7. Feeding Habits and Adaptations

1. David E. Fastovsky and David B. Weishampel, *The Evolution and Extinction of the Dinosaurs* (New York: Cambridge University Press, 1996), pp. 124–125.

2. Ibid., p. 126.

3. Robert T. Bakker, *The Dinosaur Heresies* (New York: William Morrow and Company, 1986), pp. 187–190; R. McNeill Alexander, *Dynamics of Dinosaurs and Other Extinct Giants* (New York: Columbia University Press, 1989) pp. 63–64.

4. Fastovsky and Weishampel, pp. 147–148.

5. Ibid. p. 162.

6. James O. Farlow and Michael K. Brett-Surman, eds., *The Complete Dinosaur* (Bloomington: Indiana University Press, 1997), pp. 354–360.

7. Ibid. p. 359.

Chapter 8. Armor, Clubs, Spikes, and Plates—The Decorations of Defense

1. Kenneth Carpenter, *Eggs, Nests, and Baby Dinosaurs* (Bloomington, Ind.: Indiana University Press, 1999), pp. 74–75.

2. James O. Farlow and Michael K. Brett-Surman, eds., *The Complete Dinosaur* (Bloomington: Indiana University Press, 1997), p. 315.

Chapter 9. Extinction of the Dinosaurs

1. David M. Raup, *Extinction: Bad Genes or Bad Luck?* (New York: W. W. Norton, 1991), pp. 3–4.

2. Ibid., p. 71.

Chapter 10. Major Discoveries

1. Personal communication with Kenneth Carpenter, August 24, 2000.

2. Ibid.

3. Ibid.

GLOSSARY

angiosperms—The flowering plants, the last of the major plant groups to evolve.

Archosauria—A subclass of Reptilia including crocodilians, dinosaurs (with birds), pterosaurs, and thecodonts.

bilateral symmetry—A feature of vertebrate body design in which one side of the body is a mirror image of the other.

bipedal—Walking on two legs.

braincase—The internal portion of the skull that encloses and protects the brain.

brow horn—A horn above the eye.

carnivore—A meat-eating creature.

cast—To make an exact replica of the original using a mold.

caudal—Pertaining to the tail.

Ceratopsian—"Horned face." The family of horned dinosaurs including the psittacosaurs, protoceratopsids, and ceratopsids.

cervical—Pertaining to the neck.

chordate—Animals with backbones, including those with the precursor of the backbone called the notochord.

classification—A traditional system of classifying organisms based on their similarities in form. The hierarchy of this classification method is kingdom, phylum, class, order, family, genus, species.

coprolite—Fossilized animal dung.

Cretaceous Period—The third and final major time division (144 to 65 million years ago) of the Mesozoic Era. The end of the age of dinosaurs.

ectotherm—Any of the cold-blooded animals whose body temperature is affected by the temperature of their environment and their behavior. They may actually become warmer than the air temperature while basking in full sunlight. Modern ectotherms include most fish, reptiles, and amphibians.

endotherm—Any of the warm-blooded animals that generate their own body heat internally. They have a constant body temperature no matter what the temperature of their surroundings. Modern endotherms include mammals, birds, and some fish.

evolution—The patterns of change through time of living organisms.

extinction—The irreversible elimination of an entire species of plant or animal.

femur—The long, large bone of the upper leg.

fibula—One of the two lower bones in the hind limb; the other is the tibia.

frill—A bony extension of the skull covering the neck area of protoceratopsids and ceratopsids.

growth series—A set of skeletons for a given kind of dinosaur showing various stages of growth. A growth series allows a scientist to study changes to the dinosaur as it matured and to estimate how long it took to reach adulthood.

gymnosperms—Primitive seed plants found in two groups, the conifers and the cycads.

herbivore—A plant-eating creature.

iguanodont—A member of the group of ornithopod dinosaurs including *Iguanodon.*

Jurassic Period—The second of the three major time divisions (208 to 144 million years ago) of the Mesozoic Era.

Mesozoic Era—The time of the dinosaurs (245 to 65 million years ago).

mosasaur—An aquatic fish-eating reptile with a deep, flat-sided tail.

olfactory—Pertaining to the sense of smell.

optic—Pertaining to vision.

Ornithischia—One of two groups of dinosaurs based on hip structure. Ornithischians had a hip with a backward-pointing pubis bone.

ornithopods—A group of two-footed, plant-eating, ornithischian dinosaurs.

paleontologist—A scientist who studies life-forms of the geologic past, especially through the analysis of plant and animal fossils.

pelvis—The hipbones.

plesiosaur—A large aquatic reptile of the Mesozoic Era that had a squat body, paddles as limbs, and either a long neck and small head or a short neck and big head.

predator—A creature that kills other creatures for food.

pteridophytes—Early primitive plants including ferns, horse-tails, and club mosses that had roots, stems, and leaves but no flowers or seeds.

pterosaur—A flying reptile that lived during the Mesozoic Era.

quadrupedal—Walking on four legs.

Saurischia—One of two orders of dinosaurs based on hip structure. Saurischians had a hip with a forward-pointing pubis bone.

sauropod—Any of the large, plant-eating saurischian dinosaurs with long necks and long tails.

scute—One of many flat or bony plates forming the protective covering of an armored dinosaur.

sexual dimorphism—Differences between males and females of the same kind of animal in their size, shape, physiology, and behavior.

thecodont—An order of reptiles from the Triassic Period from which evolved crocodiles, pterosaurs, dinosaurs, and birds.

theropod—Any of a group of saurischian dinosaurs that ate meat and walked on two legs.

tibia—One of the two lower bones in the hind limb; the other is the fibula.

Triassic Period—The first of the three major time divisions (245 to 208 million years ago) of the Mesozoic Era.

vertebra—A bone of the neck, spine, or tail.

vertebrate—Any animal that has a backbone (spine).

FURTHER READING

Even though there have been hundreds of books about dinosaurs published, reputable dinosaur books are hard to find. Listed here are some of the authors' favorites. They range from the examination of individual kinds of dinosaurs to several encyclopedic volumes covering a wide range of dinosaur-related topics. A number of history books are included in the list as well to help those who are interested in the lives and times of paleontologists.

Bakker, Robert T. *The Dinosaur Heresies*. New York: William Morrow and Company, 1986.

Carpenter, Kenneth. *Eggs, Nests, and Baby Dinosaurs*. Bloomington: Indiana University Press, 1999.

Colbert, Edwin H. *The Great Dinosaur Hunters and Their Discoveries*. New York: Dover Publications, 1984.

Dixon, Dougal, Barry Cox, R. J. G. Savage, and Brian Gardiner. *The Macmillan Illustrated Encyclopedia of Dinosaurs and Other Prehistoric Animals*. New York: Macmillan, 1988.

Farlow, James O., and Michael K. Brett-Surman, eds. *The Complete Dinosaur*. Bloomington: Indiana University Press, 1997.

Gallagher, William B. *When Dinosaurs Roamed New Jersey*. New Brunswick, N.J.: Rutgers University Press, 1997.

Holmes, Thom. *Fossil Feud: The Rivalry of the First American Dinosaur Hunters*. Parsippany, N.J.: Julian Messner, 1998.

Horner, John R., and James Gorman. *Digging Dinosaurs.* New York: Workman, 1988.

Norell, Mark A., Eugene S. Gaffney, and Lowell Dingus. *Discovering Dinosaurs.* New York: Alfred A. Knopf, 1995.

Norman, David. *The Illustrated Encyclopedia of Dinosaurs.* London: Salamander Books, 1985.

Russell, Dale A. *The Dinosaurs of North America: An Odyssey in Time.* Minocqua, Wisc.: NorthWord Press, 1989.

Spalding, David A. *Dinosaur Hunters.* Rocklin, Calif.: Prima Publishing, 1993.

Sternberg, Charles H. *Life of a Fossil Hunter.* New York: Dover, 1990.

Weishampel, David B., and Luther Young. *Dinosaurs of the East Coast.* Baltimore: Johns Hopkins University Press, 1996.

INTERNET ADDRESSES

American Museum of Natural History. *Fossil Halls.* <http://www.amnh.org/exhibitions/Fossil_Halls/index.html>.

Jacobson, Russ. *Dino Russ's Lair: Dinosaur and Vertebrate Paleontology Information.* March 14, 2001. <http://www.isgs.uiuc.edu/dinos/dinos_home.html>.

National Geographic Society. *Dinosaur Eggs.* © 1996. <http://www.nationalgeographic.com/dinoeggs/>.

The Natural History Museum, London. *Dinosaur Data Files.* © 1994–2001. <http://www.nhm.ac.uk/education/online/dinosaur_data_files.html>.

The Royal Tyrrell Museum of Palaeontology, Alberta. *Dinosaur Hall.* © 1995–1997. <http://www.tyrrellmuseum.com/peek/index2.php?strSection=6>.

Scotese, Christopher R. *Paleomap Project.* February 19, 2001. <http://www.scotese.com>.

Smithsonian Institute. *Department of Paleontology.* n.d. <http://www.nmnh.si.edu/paleo/index.html>.

Summer, Edward. *The Dinosaur Interplanetary Gazette.* January 12, 2001. <http://www.dinosaur.org/frontpage.html>.

University of Bristol. *Dinobase.* n.d. <http://palaeo.gly.bris.ac.uk/dinobase/dinopage.html>.

University of California, Berkeley, Museum of Paleontology. *The Dinosauria: Truth Is Stranger Than Fiction.* © 1994–2001. <http://www.ucmp.berkeley.edu/diapsids/dinosaur.html>.

INDEX